The Adventure Begins

THE
Adventure
═BEGINS═

KIT SUBLETT

Whitecaps Media
Houston

Whitecaps Media
Houston, Texas
whitecapsmedia.com

ISBN: 978-0-9883628-3-3

FIRST EDITION

For information on bulk purchases of this book, please visit whitecapsmedia.com

Printed in the United States of America

Dedicated to my mom

Ruth Allyn Whitlock Sublett

whose own example of
unconditional love and grace
made it easy for all of her children
to believe in God's

READ THIS FIRST!

This book has been written to help you get started in your walk with Christ—the greatest adventure life has to offer!

My hope is for you to solidify what you have already learned about Christ and begin taking positive steps in your relationship with Him.

Don't read this book all in one sitting. The best way to read it is one chapter a day for the next few weeks. Enjoy!

FIRST DAY

Congratulations!

If you're reading this book it means you have decided, perhaps for the very first time, to follow Christ. You're in for the ride of your life!

You and I were designed by God to have fellowship with Him, and until we do that, we're not living life the way it ought to be lived—"abundantly" as Jesus tells us in John 10:10.

For years I worked with a ministry to high school students called Young Life. Its founder, Jim Rayburn, used to say if you don't know Christ, you're not living, you're just moving. Now, though, you're prepared to start *living*. This little book will help you make a good start to your new life in Christ.

A good place to start would be a review of some of the basics of the gospel. Paul, a man who had a dramatic turnaround for Christ (like you may have had), became one of the greatest Christians who ever lived. He wrote these words to a young man who, like you, had decided to follow Jesus:

> But when the goodness and loving
> kindness of God our Savior appeared,

he saved us, not because of works done
by us in righteousness, but according
to his own mercy, by the washing of
regeneration and renewal of the Holy
Spirit, whom he poured out on us richly
through Jesus Christ our Savior, so that
being justified by his grace we might
become heirs according to the hope of
eternal life. The saying is trustworthy,
and I want you to insist on these things,
so that those who have believed in God
may be careful to devote themselves to
good works. These things are excellent
and profitable for people. (Titus 3:4–8)

Let's take a look at that first part: "But when
the goodness and loving kindness of God our
Savior appeared, he saved us, not because of works
done by us in righteousness, but according to his
own mercy."

God appeared to us in the Person of Jesus
Christ—the greatest, most wonderful person who
ever lived. As one writer has put it, Jesus was "God
with skin on"—God's own Son, come to earth. If
you want to know what God is like, look at Jesus.
When Christ came to earth and walked among
us, we were given a chance to see what God is like
up close. And is He ever incredible! He's the only

person about whom you cannot exaggerate—you can't say enough good things about Christ. It's impossible! Read through the Gospels (the first four books of the New Testament in your Bible) and see if you can find any fault with Jesus—you can't! He was kind, He was loving; He was rugged, strong, compassionate, and smart. He had integrity, He was wise, He loved to help other people. And, oh yeah, He was God. "God among us" (*Emmanuel* in Hebrew) was even one of His names.

But it gets even better.

You see, He didn't just leave heaven and come to our planet to show us what God is like (although that would have still ranked as the greatest event in history). Paul reminds us in Titus that Jesus saved us.

"Saved us from what?" you might ask. The Bible tells us that Jesus saved us from the punishment that our sin rightly deserves.

In order to be God, God cannot put up with sin. He must be morally perfect. We wouldn't want Him any other way. We want and need God to be just and to always do the right thing. If He was less than that, He wouldn't be any different than we are. The problem, though, is that for Him to be perfect He cannot tolerate sin. Sin must be punished. Again, we want that: We want God to punish wrongdoers and to bring justice to bear on the pain and suffering that we have endured or that our loved ones have endured. We don't want God to just look the other way at sin (unless, of course, it's our own sin).

And therein lies the problem. And it's not just a problem for us, this idea that we must be punished for going against God's will. It's also a problem for God Himself. You see, God made you and He made me. He made us for a relationship with Himself. It breaks His heart that we have turned our backs on Him and that we have brought this separation between Him and us. God loves us desperately, but He cannot tolerate the sin in our lives. He cannot just look the other way.

That's where Jesus comes in. He was the perfect go-between. Because He was both God and Man, He was able to bridge the gap. Romans 5:6 tells us that "at the right time Christ died for the ungodly" (that's you and me). Being Man He could represent us; being God He had no sin of His own for which to pay. So when Christ went to the cross it was not for Himself: it was to pay the price that otherwise you and I would have to pay for our own sin. And God the Father accepted the payment that God the Son (Jesus) made on our behalf.

The great British preacher Richard Bewes wrote, "It is one small step that is required ... at the foot of a Roman cross. It is the only place where God will meet us."

I hope that you have received Christ's gift for yourself. If not, you can do so now. Receiving God's gift is a simple matter of believing.

Again, the verses from Titus are a good summary: "[Jesus] saved us, not because of works done by us in righteousness, but according to his own mercy." You see, it is a gift—we don't earn it through righteous or good things that we do. Instead Jesus gives us this because of His mercy. "Mercy" is a word we've all heard before but maybe don't know what it means. To have mercy on someone means to *not* give them what they deserve. We deserved to be punished for our sins (and death—eternal separation from God—is what the punishment is), but through Christ's own death on the cross God is willing to have mercy upon us and to show favor to us. A great verse that sums this up is Romans 6:23: "For the wages of sin is death, but the free gift of God is eternal life in Christ Jesus our Lord."

How do we receive that gift? By accepting it; that is, by placing our trust in Christ.

When I was young, I used to love Christmas (what kid doesn't?). And of course, it wasn't the birth of Christ that got me excited about that holiday; it was the gifts under the tree that were for me! There they were, all wrapped up with an air of mystery about them and some with my name on them. Those gifts were meant for me! And without fail every December 25 I would open each and every one of them and receive them and use them.

But just because a gift was wrapped, addressed to me, and placed under the tree didn't mean that I had received it yet. It was only when I appropriated it (which is a fancy word that means to take for yourself, or to open the gift) that it truly became mine. In the same way, God's gift of salvation and eternal life through Christ is there for you. The gift has been purchased (through Christ's blood). It's got your name on it (He died for you). And it's been placed under the tree (you have been told about the gift now). All that remains is for you to receive it or appropriate it for yourself.

We do that by faith.

John 1:12 tells us that "to all who did receive him, who believed in his name, he gave the right to become children of God." Here's my paraphrase of that verse: "To everyone who receives Christ by faith, that is, everyone who believes in who Jesus is and what He has done, God gives the right to become His children."

Have you placed your trust in Christ? You can do that right now if you haven't already done so. Just pray a simple prayer to Christ:

Jesus, I believe that You exist and that You are able to hear me right now. I know that I have done wrong and sinned against You. I'm truly sorry for that, Lord. I'm sorry that I have turned my back on You in so many ways. But I know and believe that You are who You said You are—the Son of God—and that You came here to give me a second chance. I believe that You died on the cross to pay for my sins, and I put my full trust and faith in You—and nothing else—for eternal life. I know, Lord, that I don't deserve anything on my own, but that You have paid the price in full for

*me. Please enter into my heart right now
and begin to live life in and through me. In
Christ's name, Amen.*

When you sincerely place your faith in Christ
(as that prayer expresses) God forgives you of your
sin and welcomes you into His family. It could be
through that prayer, or it could be that you placed
your faith in Christ at an earlier time. What matters most is *believing right* about Christ.

Most of this might have been a review for
you. But I wanted to make sure that you had a
good understanding of what the basic gospel
message is. Someone once said that if a Christian
can't explain what he believes he may not be a
Christian. That's because Christianity is based on
what you believe about Christ. If you can't explain
those beliefs then maybe you don't truly believe
them. A Christian is someone who believes right
about Jesus Christ.

If you have begun to "believe right" about
Him, to believe what the Bible has to say about
Christ and about life, then you are ready to begin
to live life as God intended it to be lived. Let the
adventure begin!

DAY 2

If you go to Europe you will undoubtedly see the great churches of St. Peter's in Rome and St. Paul's in London. They are some of the most beautiful and significant buildings in the world. If you travel on into Russia, you might visit the beautiful city of St. Petersburg. I was born in St. Luke's Hospital in Houston; also in Houston is St. John's, one of the finest high schools in the state. Are you noticing something they all have in common? They're all named for tax collectors and fishermen who lived in the first century AD. I could go on and on: almost every town and neighborhood in America has something—a school, a church, a hospital—named after one of these men who lived over 2,000 years ago.

Why?

Not because they were great fishermen (how many other first-century fishermen can you name?). Nor because they were particularly clever or wealthy. *It is because they followed Christ.*

Christ made them great, and He wants to make you great as well.

The rest of this book is devoted to helping you begin that adventure, or as Paul said to Titus, "that those who have believed in God may be careful to devote themselves to good works. These things are excellent and profitable."

When those men—Peter, John, Luke, Paul, and the others—began to follow Christ their lives changed in many ways. Yours, too, will change in many of the same ways as you follow Christ.

The early believers began to understand life much better, so much so that the words they wrote have inspired millions more in the centuries that have followed. You, too, will begin to understand life as never before. Why? Because now you know the One who made life and who made you!

Jesus said, "This is eternal life, that they know you the only true God, and Jesus Christ whom you have sent" (John 17:3). Life is all tied up in knowing Jesus. As you get to know Him better, as the disciples did, you will understand life better and have a proper understanding of yourself as well.

The first followers of Jesus also began to have a purpose. Simply stated, it was to know Christ and to make Him known to others. Because of that they turned the world upside down! Think about it: You and I have faith in Christ now, some

2,000 years later, due in large part to their efforts to make sure that Jesus' message spread to others. Wouldn't it be great to have a life that impacted others—for eternity? Well, you too have a purpose now, and it's the same one as theirs was: to know Christ yourself and to make Him known to others. You can turn your world upside down, starting with your friends, your school or workplace, and your family.

In Matthew 22 we read about a man who came to Jesus and asked Him, "Teacher, which is the great commandment in the Law?" Jesus responded to him with words that tell us what is most important for all of us: "You shall love the Lord your God with all your heart and with all your soul and with all your mind." That becomes our new purpose, our new marching orders. Whatever God wants us to do, that's what we should do. He wants us to know Him personally and spend time with Him. In doing that—in loving Him—He will slowly and surely change our hearts, our minds, and every aspect of our lives.

Another exciting change that happened to those first- century believers was that they received a peace of mind and a courage that they had never known before. When you read the accounts of

Jesus' crucifixion, you will see that the disciples hardly showed courage; far from it—they all ran away from Christ when things got dangerous. But then an amazing thing happened. Christ rose from the dead and appeared to the disciples. He gave His followers the Holy Spirit. Then those same men who ran rather than face danger became different men. Tradition tells us that almost all of them met their deaths rather than give up their belief in Christ. Most of them at some point in their lives were arrested, beaten, stranded, tried in court, hounded, misunderstood, or persecuted for what he believed.

Yet they wouldn't give up!

In fact, in the middle of being imprisoned for sharing the same news that you have recently heard, Paul wrote this verse (Philippians 4:7): "And the peace of God, which surpasses all understanding, will guard your hearts and your minds in Christ Jesus."

Even in the midst of difficult times the early followers of Christ enjoyed God's peace, which only comes through knowing Jesus. This will happen to you, too. As you follow hard after Christ, no matter what else happens in your life, you will be able to experience the courage, the peace, and the joy of life that is only available through knowing Jesus.

As you may have picked up reading that last part, not all of the changes that happened in the early believers' lives were pleasant. Like I said, almost all of them were persecuted and mistreated for believing in Christ. One of Jesus' early followers was a man named Legion (you can read his story in Mark 5). Legion had lots of problems and when Jesus healed him the people who knew Legion had an interesting response: They were afraid of him and how his life had changed! You may experience this as well. I have certainly known plenty of high school guys and girls who came home from Young Life camp after deciding to follow Christ only to have their friends back home desert them.

Why do they do that?

I think it's similar to what happened to Legion: your friends may be afraid of the change that has happened in your life. People are naturally scared of what they don't understand, and, unless they know Christ, too, all this change in your life may be threatening to them. (My suggestion to you is to keep loving them, and pray that they, too, will come to know Christ as you are now doing.)

But let me encourage you with this thought: While some friends no doubt deserted the early followers of Jesus, some other things were happening—enemies became brothers, and friendships became more intense, meaningful, and deep. This is going to happen to you as well. Walking with Christ you are going to meet people you never imagined would become your friends. And they will become dear brothers and sisters in the faith who will enrich your life immeasurably. God is going to bless you with wonderful friends as you follow Him!

Finally, as you get serious about Christ, life will be of better quality than ever before, but this may come at a price.

I think of a guy I met working at a Young Life camp. I asked him his story. Just a year earlier he had dropped out of high school and was selling drugs, making more money than his father did. But along the way, he had come to trust Christ the same way you have and he left that former life behind. Now here he was, working long hours every day for no pay behind the scenes at a Christian camp. A year earlier he had all the money, girls, and drugs he wanted. He was "somebody."

I asked him which was better, life before Christ or life since Christ.

He laughed.

"There's no comparison. I'd take my worst day as a Christian any day over my best day in my previous life." When he had first accepted Christ he was persecuted severely: his former drug contacts literally wanted to see him dead. But with God's help and the help of some brothers and sisters in Christ, he persevered and was experiencing things that his previous lifestyle could not afford: peace, purpose, and security in Christ.

I think, too, of another young man I met many years ago at the same camp. He was from Asia, from a country without many Christians. Knowing that, I asked how he had become a believer. He had come to America to go to college and while in school had met some students who were Christians. They became his friends and eventually led him to Christ.

I asked him how his parents, who were not believers, had responded. "Not very well," he told me sadly. "They said that if I do not reject my new beliefs they will disown me."

I saw him a year later, once again working at camp and pursuing his relationship with Christ.

"How did it go with your parents?" I asked hopefully. "Not well," he said. His parents had indeed disowned him—he was no longer their son, they said. But even with that heartbreak he knew he would not turn his back on Christ. Instead he was going to do whatever it took to see that his parents became Christians.

Paul, a follower of Christ who had no shortage of heartache in his own life, said it this way: "For to me to live is Christ, and to die is gain" (Philippians 1:21).

Life with Christ is a great adventure. There will be wonderful new blessings in your life—new friends, new interests, new perspectives, new joy. There may also be some tough times ahead. But in all of that, good and bad, you now have the wonderful promise of God Himself: "I will never leave you nor forsake you" (Hebrews 13:5). He will make your life all that it is meant to be.

So what are the first steps you need to take in this journey? Here are two I would encourage you to take:

First, tell a Christian friend or pastor about your decision to follow Christ. You'll need their support as you begin to walk with Christ. Additionally, it will help you solidify things if you tell someone about your decision. Just tell them, "I've decided to put my trust in Christ and have become a Christian." That's all you need to say.

Second, get a Bible that you can understand easily. Before you put down your money for a Bible, take a look at it and read a few passages. Is it easy to read? Are there lots of "thee's" and "thou's"? You probably don't want that one as it will be hard to understand. The translation I use in this book is the English Standard Version and I highly recommend it.

Whichever translation you get, know this: the Bible is God's love letter to you. It will change your life if you make a regular habit of reading it and apply its teaching.

Our next section will talk a little more about how to read the Bible. Read it tomorrow (the next section, that is, not the entire Bible!).

DAY 3

The remaining chapters of this book can be used as daily devotionals or "Quiet Times." A Quiet Time is nothing more than spending some time with your new best friend, Jesus.

Some folks like to have their devotional the first thing in the morning, others like to do so as they go to bed at night. For me, the middle of the day has often been the best time to slow down and have a Quiet Time. You know, it really doesn't matter *when* you spend time with the Lord; what matters is that you *do* it!

Someone once asked my friend John, "How often should I read the Bible?" And he replied, "How often do you want to hear from God?" That would be my response, too. You should get in the habit of regularly spending time with Christ, because surely you want to hear from Him daily.

So how does one go about having a daily devotional? Let me suggest two key components. The first is God's Word, and the second is prayer. The two go hand in hand, and in this chapter we're going to take a look at each of them.

Do you have a Bible? If you do, make sure it's easy to understand. If it isn't, get one that is. The English Standard Version (ESV), which I recommend, has an excellent eBook version for your mobile device and it's sometimes available free of charge. But you'll also want a paper version. Any bookstore will carry a variety of Bibles, including some that you'll find very affordable. Get one.

You might think the place to start reading the Bible is on page 1 at Genesis, chapter 1. Let me encourage you *not* to do that! Instead, begin with the book of Mark in the New Testament. Why? Because Mark is all about Jesus, the One you now have a relationship with, and it's action-packed. You'll find it easy and interesting to read.

How much should you read? I suggest a chapter a day. There may come a time when you will want to read more; conversely there may be a time when you want to really dig into just a paragraph or two. But day in and day out, a chapter of the New Testament is a good length.

Prior to becoming a Christian you may have tried to read the Bible and found it to be dull or difficult to understand. My prediction is that now neither of those will be true. If you have a good, easy to read version (like the ESV or the New

Living Translation), you'll find the Bible to be very accessible and understandable. But more than the translation, the fact that you have a relationship with the Author will make reading the Bible more interesting. As someone once told me, the Bible is God's love letter to His children; when you try to read it before you are a Christian it's like reading someone else's mail, and therefore hard to understand.

Reading the Bible is absolutely essential to the Christian experience. We need to hear from Christ what He wants us to do with our lives and how He wants us to live, respond, react, and behave.

One of the greatest Christians who ever lived was a man named George Müller. He wrote,

> The vigor of our spiritual life will be in exact proportion to the place held by the Bible in our life and thoughts. I solemnly state this from the experience of fifty-four years.
>
> The first three years after conversion I neglected the Word of God. Since I began to search it diligently the blessing has been wonderful.
>
> I have read the Bible through one hundred times, and always with increasing

delight. Each time it seems like a new book to me.

Great has been the blessing from consecutive, diligent, daily study. I look upon it as a lost day when I have not had a good time over the Word of God.

You'll begin your own study of God's Word by reading the first chapter of the Gospel of Mark in just a moment. But first we need to talk a little about prayer.

Scripture is God's primary way of speaking to us and prayer is our primary way of speaking to God. What's on your mind? What's troubling you? What things are going on in your life? What are you thankful for? God wants to hear from you about all of these things.

There are many ways to pray and I'll give you examples of a few different ways in the Quiet Times in this book. But the main thing is to tell the Lord what's on your heart, including confessing to Him the things you've done that you shouldn't have.

I often begin my prayer time by thanking God for the good things in my life. Then I might go on to spend a little time thinking through the previous day and confessing my sins and getting right with God. Then I love to bring before the Lord all the concerns of my day: prayers for my family and friends, for my church, requests for our nation and for my work, and anything else that comes to mind.

I'll close this section with another quote from George Müller:

> It is a common temptation of Satan to make us give up reading the Word and prayer when our enjoyment is gone; as if it were of no use to read the Scriptures when we do not enjoy them, and as if it were no use to pray when we have no spirit of prayer. The truth is that, in order to enjoy the Word, we ought to continue to read it, and the way to obtain a spirit of prayer is to continue praying. The less we read the Word of God, the less we desire to read it, and the less we pray, the less we desire to pray.

Begin the habit of having a daily devotional now. You will never regret it. Let's start with reading Mark.

QUIET TIME

Read Mark 1 below and answer the questions that follow.

---

1 THE BEGINNING OF the gospel of Jesus Christ, the Son of God.

2 ¶ As it is written in Isaiah the prophet,

> "Behold, I send my messenger
>   before your face,
>   who will prepare your way,
> **3**   the voice of one crying in the
>   wilderness:
>   'Prepare the way of the Lord,
>   make his paths straight,'"

4 ¶ John appeared, baptizing in the wilderness and proclaiming a baptism of repentance for the forgiveness of sins.

5 And all the country of Judea and all Jerusalem were going out to him and were being baptized by him in the river Jordan, confessing their sins.

6 Now John was clothed with camel's hair and wore a leather belt around his waist and ate locusts and wild honey.

7 And he preached, saying, "After me comes he who is mightier than I, the strap of whose sandals I am not worthy to stoop down and untie.

8 I have baptized you with water, but he will baptize

you with the Holy Spirit."

⁹ ¶ In those days Jesus came from Nazareth of Galilee and was baptized by John in the Jordan.

¹⁰ And when he came up out of the water, immediately he saw the heavens opening and the Spirit descending on him like a dove.

¹¹ And a voice came from heaven, "You are my beloved Son; with you I am well pleased."

¹² ¶ The Spirit immediately drove him out into the wilderness.

¹³ And he was in the wilderness forty days, being tempted by Satan. And he was with the wild animals, and the angels were ministering to him.

¹⁴ ¶ Now after John was arrested, Jesus came into Galilee, proclaiming the gospel of God,

¹⁵ and saying, "The time is fulfilled, and the kingdom of God is at hand; repent and believe in the gospel."

¹⁶ ¶ Passing alongside the Sea of Galilee, he saw Simon and Andrew the brother of Simon casting a net into the sea, for they were fishermen.

¹⁷ And Jesus said to them, "Follow me, and I will make you become fishers of men."

¹⁸ And immediately they left their nets and followed him.

¹⁹ And going on a little farther, he saw James the son of Zebedee and John his brother, who were in their boat mending the nets.

²⁰ And immediately he called them, and they left their father Zebedee in the boat with the hired servants and followed him.

²¹ ¶ And they went into Capernaum, and immediately on the Sabbath he entered the synagogue and was teaching.

²² And they were astonished at his teaching, for he taught them as one who had authority, and not as the scribes.

²³ And immediately there was in their synagogue a man with an unclean spirit. And he cried out,

²⁴ "What have you to do with us, Jesus of Nazareth? Have you come to destroy us? I know who you are— the Holy One of God."

²⁵ But Jesus rebuked him, saying, "Be silent, and come out of him!"

²⁶ And the unclean spirit, convulsing him and crying out with a loud voice, came out of him.

²⁷ And they were all amazed, so that they questioned among themselves, saying, "What is this? A new teaching with authority! He commands even the un- clean spirits, and they obey him."

²⁸ And at once his fame spread everywhere through- out all the surrounding region of Galilee.

²⁹ ¶ And immediately he left the synagogue and entered the house of Simon and Andrew, with James and John.

³⁰ Now Simon's mother-in-law lay ill with a fever, and immediately they told him about her.

³¹ And he came and took her by the hand and lifted her up, and the fever left her, and she began to serve them.

³² ¶ That evening at sundown they brought to him all who were sick or oppressed by demons.

³³ And the whole city was gathered together at the door.

³⁴ And he healed many who were sick with various diseases, and cast out many demons. And he would not permit the demons to speak, because they knew him.

³⁵ ¶ And rising very early in the morning, while it was still dark, he departed and went out to a desolate place, and there he prayed.

³⁶ And Simon and those who were with him searched for him,

³⁷ and they found him and said to him, "Everyone is looking for you."

³⁸ And he said to them, "Let us go on to the next towns, that I may preach there also, for that is why I came out."

³⁹ And he went throughout all Galilee, preaching in their synagogues and casting out demons.

⁴⁰ ¶ And a leper came to him, imploring him, and

kneeling said to him, "If you will, you can make me clean."

⁴¹ Moved with pity, he stretched out his hand and touched him and said to him, "I will; be clean."

⁴² And immediately the leprosy left him, and he was made clean.

⁴³ And Jesus sternly charged him and sent him away at once,

⁴⁴ and said to him, "See that you say nothing to anyone, but go, show yourself to the priest and offer for your cleansing what Moses commanded, for a proof to them."

⁴⁵ But he went out and began to talk freely about it, and to spread the news, so that Jesus could no longer openly enter a town, but was out in desolate places, and people were coming to him from every quarter.

QUESTIONS

1. What does verse 11 tell us about Jesus?

2. Why do you think Simon and Andrew "left their nets" and followed Christ? What are you "leaving" to follow Christ?

3. Do you think Simon, Andrew, James, and John were glad they followed Christ? Why?

4. In verse 31 Simon's mother-in-law is healed and begins to serve Christ. How can you serve Christ this day?

5. What is Jesus doing in verse 35? (Answer: He's having a Quiet Time. You're in good company!)

Hugh Silvester said, "One of the saddest things about the atheist is that he has no one to thank." But that's not true for you and me! So spend some time thanking God for what He has done for you. List ten things or people you can think of and take a moment to reflect on each one and thank the Lord for them:

1. _____

2. _____

3. _____

4. _____

5. _____

6. _____

7. _____

8. _____

9. _____

10. _____

In Mark 1:23–26 Christ got rid of the man's evil spirits. What would you like for Him to remove or change in your life? Ask Him to do so now.

Spend some time praying for the needs of your family.

Spend some time praying for your friends.

Close your time with Christ by thanking Him again for paying the cost for your sins and asking Him to help you to follow Him today.

DAY 4

One of my favorite things about being a Christian is the quality and quantity of friends the Lord gives to me. He has put the most incredible, exciting, funny, courageous, beautiful, and amazing people in my life. Being with other Christians is called fellowship, and now you're a part of that fellowship of believers.

Your walk with Christ will be immensely improved by spending time with other Christians. In many ways Christianity is no different than any other relationship: You get to know a new friend by talking with each other one-on-one, by doing things together, and through spending time together with mutual friends.

An example may help. I have a good friend named Luis. When we talk with one another our friendship is strengthened (just like having a Quiet Time strengthens your friendship with the Lord). When we don't spend time with each other the friendship suffers, so we make an effort to stay in touch (as we should make an effort to have a Quiet Time). But in addition to those times talking just to Luis, it also helps for me to spend time with Luis and his wife Jill. Getting to know Jill is not only great because I strengthen my friendship with her, but because I also get to know Luis better through her.

In the same way, when you spend time with other believers you will learn about Christ. Why? Because just like Jill knows her husband better than I do, your Christian friends may show you a side to Christ that you didn't know before. Additionally, fellowship will encourage you. It can also hold you "accountable" or responsible for your actions.

Another important thing about fellowship is that you can help your brothers and sisters in Christ; it's a two-way street! And when you neglect to spend time in fellowship, they miss out on what you can give to them.

Lastly, we are called to worship God with other believers, not just by ourselves. You need to get involved in a church. Get in the habit of going every Sunday. You may not always enjoy it, but your participation is important for you and for your church.

Day 4

QUIET TIME

Begin your QT today by reading Mark 2, then
answer the questions that follow.

---

2 ¶ AND WHEN [Jesus] returned to Capernaum
after some days, it was reported that he was at
home.

² And many were gathered together, so that there
was no more room, not even at the door. And he was
preaching the word to them.

³ And they came, bringing to him a paralytic carried
by four men.

⁴ And when they could not get near him because of
the crowd, they removed the roof above him, and
when they had made an opening, they let down the
bed on which the paralytic lay.

⁵ And when Jesus saw their faith, he said to the paralytic, "My son, your sins are forgiven."

⁶ Now some of the scribes were sitting there, ques-
tioning in their hearts,

⁷ "Why does this man speak like that? He is blas-
pheming! Who can forgive sins but God alone?"

⁸ And immediately Jesus, perceiving in his spirit that
they thus questioned within themselves, said to them,
"Why do you question these things in your hearts?

⁹ Which is easier, to say to the paralytic, 'Your sins are forgiven,' or to say, 'Rise, take up your bed and walk'?

¹⁰ But that you may know that the Son of Man has authority on earth to forgive sins"—he said to the paralytic—

¹¹ "I say to you, rise, pick up your bed, and go home."

¹² And he rose and immediately picked up his bed and went out before them all, so that they were all amazed and glorified God, saying, "We never saw anything like this!"

¹³ ¶ He went out again beside the sea, and all the crowd was coming to him, and he was teaching them.

¹⁴ And as he passed by, he saw Levi the son of Alphaeus sitting at the tax booth, and he said to him, "Follow me." And he rose and followed him.

¹⁵ ¶ And as he reclined at table in his house, many tax collectors and sinners were reclining with Jesus and his disciples, for there were many who followed him.

¹⁶ And the scribes of the Pharisees, when they saw that he was eating with sinners and tax collectors, said to his disciples, "Why does he eat with tax collectors and sinners?"

¹⁷ And when Jesus heard it, he said to them, "Those who are well have no need of a physician, but those

who are sick. I came not to call the righteous, but sinners."

¹⁸ ¶ Now John's disciples and the Pharisees were fasting. And people came and said to him, "Why do John's disciples and the disciples of the Pharisees fast, but your disciples do not fast?"

¹⁹ And Jesus said to them, "Can the wedding guests fast while the bridegroom is with them? As long as they have the bridegroom with them, they cannot fast.

²⁰ The days will come when the bridegroom is taken away from them, and then they will fast in that day.

²¹ No one sews a piece of unshrunk cloth on an old garment. If he does, the patch tears away from it, the new from the old, and a worse tear is made.

²² And no one puts new wine into old wineskins. If he does, the wine will burst the skins—and the wine is destroyed, and so are the skins. But new wine is for fresh wineskins."

²³ ¶ One Sabbath he was going through the grainfields, and as they made their way, his disciples began to pluck heads of grain.

²⁴ And the Pharisees were saying to him, "Look, why are they doing what is not lawful on the Sabbath?"

²⁵ And he said to them, "Have you never read what David did, when he was in need and was hungry, he and those who were with him:

²⁶ how he entered the house of God, in the time of Abiathar the high priest, and ate the bread of the Presence, which it is not lawful for any but the priests to eat, and also gave it to those who were with him?"

²⁷ And he said to them, "The Sabbath was made for man, not man for the Sabbath.

²⁸ So the Son of Man is lord even of the Sabbath."

QUESTIONS

1. In this chapter you see lots of people coming out to see Jesus. Why were they interested in hearing Him and what He had to say? Why are you interested in following Jesus?

2. The paralytic's friends cared enough about him to bring him to the feet of Jesus. Write the names of three friends of yours that you would like to bring to Jesus. Begin praying for them daily:

1. _____

2. _____

3. _____

3. The teachers of the law are upset that Jesus tells the paralyzed man his sins are forgiven. Why would that upset them? What does the fact that Jesus forgave sins tell us about who He is?

4. In the story of Levi (vv. 13–17), why do you think Jesus was willing to go to Levi's house and have fellowship with him? Why were the teachers of the law upset that Jesus did so? Look at verse 17; what was Jesus' response to them? What did He mean by that?

Spend some time thanking the Lord for people and things you are grateful for (feel free to use yesterday's list).

Now ask for the Lord's help in the things that you are most concerned about.

If you haven't already done so, pray for the friends you listed on question two on the previous page.

Close out your time with the Lord by asking His help to follow Him today.

DAY 5

How can you tell if someone loves Jesus?

Here's how Jesus Himself answered that question: He said very simply, "If you love me, you will keep my commandments" (John 14:15).

By that measure, how do you stack up? Does your love for Jesus show itself in the way you live? Do you obey what He commands? Christians are called upon to be different from the rest of the world, but to be different in a positive way. The word "Christian" actually means "little Christ." In other words, we are to pattern our life after Christ's example and be little Jesuses for the people around us.

This is one reason why it's so important that you spend time studying Scripture. The Bible is the best way to find out what God thinks and how Jesus lived, thereby giving us concrete examples of how to live our lives.

But in addition to reading it, we need to actually apply it to our lives—to live out our faith, and to obey what God is telling us through His Word.

We've all known people who call themselves Christians but whose lives do not reflect their faith. We usually call those people "hypocrites" and they're one of the main reasons many people do not want to become Christians. The way to avoid being a hypocrite is to obey what Christ tells us.

In the book of James we read: "If anyone is a hearer of the word and not a doer, he is like a man who looks intently at his natural face in a mirror. For he looks at himself and goes away and at once forgets what he was like" (James 1:23–24). James goes on to tell us that we will be blessed when we obey God's Word.

So, what are some of those things we should do? One way to find out is to look for instruction when you read the Bible each day, and ask yourself, *Is there anything in today's reading that shows me something I need to change?* If you're reading with an open heart, you will find clear instruction every day. So read your Bible and ask God's help to apply that wisdom to your life. Don't be a hypocrite!

QUIET TIME
Begin your QT today by reading Mark 3, then answer the questions that follow.

3 ¶ AGAIN HE entered the synagogue, and a man was there with a withered hand.

² And they watched Jesus, to see whether he would heal him on the Sabbath, so that they might accuse him.

³ And he said to the man with the withered hand, "Come here."

⁴ And he said to them, "Is it lawful on the Sabbath to do good or to do harm, to save life or to kill?" But they were silent.

⁵ And he looked around at them with anger, grieved at their hardness of heart, and said to the man, "Stretch out your hand." He stretched it out, and his hand was restored.

⁶ The Pharisees went out and immediately held counsel with the Herodians against him, how to destroy him.

⁷ ¶ Jesus withdrew with his disciples to the sea, and a great crowd followed, from Galilee and Judea

⁸ and Jerusalem and Idumea and from beyond the Jordan and from around Tyre and Sidon. When the great crowd heard all that he was doing, they came to him.

⁹ And he told his disciples to have a boat ready for him because of the crowd, lest they crush him,

¹⁰ for he had healed many, so that all who had diseases pressed around him to touch him.

¹¹ And whenever the unclean spirits saw him, they fell down before him and cried out, "You are the Son of God."

¹² And he strictly ordered them not to make him known.

¹³ ¶ And he went up on the mountain and called to him those whom he desired, and they came to him.

¹⁴ And he appointed twelve (whom he also named apostles) so that they might be with him and he might send them out to preach

¹⁵ and have authority to cast out demons.

¹⁶ He appointed the twelve: Simon (to whom he gave the name Peter);

¹⁷ James the son of Zebedee and John the brother of James (to whom he gave the name Boanerges, that is, Sons of Thunder);

¹⁸ Andrew, and Philip, and Bartholomew, and Matthew, and Thomas, and James the son of Alphaeus, and Thaddaeus, and Simon the Cananaean,

¹⁹ and Judas Iscariot, who betrayed him.

²⁰ ¶ Then he went home, and the crowd gathered again, so that they could not even eat.

²¹ And when his family heard it, they went out to seize him, for they were saying, "He is out of his mind."

²² ¶ And the scribes who came down from Jerusalem were saying, "He is possessed by Beelzebul," and "by

the prince of demons he casts out the demons."

²³ And he called them to him and said to them in parables, "How can Satan cast out Satan?

²⁴ If a kingdom is divided against itself, that kingdom cannot stand.

²⁵ And if a house is divided against itself, that house will not be able to stand.

²⁶ And if Satan has risen up against himself and is divided, he cannot stand, but is coming to an end.

²⁷ But no one can enter a strong man's house and plunder his goods, unless he first binds the strong man. Then indeed he may plunder his house.

²⁸ ¶ "Truly, I say to you, all sins will be forgiven the children of man, and whatever blasphemies they utter,

²⁹ but whoever blasphemes against the Holy Spirit never has forgiveness, but is guilty of an eternal sin"—

³⁰ for they had said, "He has an unclean spirit."

³¹ ¶ And his mother and his brothers came, and standing outside they sent to him and called him.

³² And a crowd was sitting around him, and they said to him, "Your mother and your brothers are outside, seeking you."

³³ And he answered them, "Who are my mother and my brothers?"

³⁴ And looking about at those who sat around him, he said, "Here are my mother and my brothers!

³⁵ Whoever does the will of God, he is my brother and sister and mother."

QUESTIONS

1. In this chapter (especially verses 7–12) you see lots of people crowding around Jesus. What do they want from Him?

2. In the next passage (vv. 13–19) you see Jesus calling twelve people to be His disciples. What made these twelve different from the others? (Hint: It has to do with their willingness to obey Christ's commands.)

3. Jesus' own family thought He was out of His mind. What are some things Jesus said about Himself that people might find hard to believe?

4. Who does Jesus say His mother and brothers are? (Hint: it has something to do with obedience!)

As you have been walking with Christ for a few days now, what are some things that you think He might want you to do differently in your life? List some things you can do today or this week to treat people the way Christ would. Be specific—and do them!

_____

_____

_____

_____

_____

_____

End by thanking the Lord for this day!

~

How can a young man keep his way pure?
By guarding it according to your word.
With my whole heart I seek you;
let me not wander from your commandments!
—Psalm 119:9–10

DAY 6

Who was the most instrumental person in your becoming a Christian? What did he or she do that really made a difference?

One of the great privileges of being a follower of Christ is that He uses us to spread His message. We get to be part of the great adventure of winning the world to Christ. The book of Second Corinthians tells us that we are God's ambassadors—His representatives—and that He uses us to tell others about Him (2 Corinthians 5:20–21).

A lot of times we think that the job of telling others about Christ is best left to the "professionals," like preachers and evangelists. But that's not what the Bible says. It says *we* are the ones who are supposed to do the job.

You don't need to have all the answers to begin telling people about Christ, nor do you have to be particularly eloquent. What matters most is your willingness to be used by the Lord.

I think of my friend Tom and his daughter. When she was in elementary school she forgot her lunch one day. Tom didn't have any appointments that morning and jumped at the opportunity to take the lunch to his daughter's school. When he arrived the little girl insisted on grabbing her father's hand and leading him down the halls of the school. "This is my daddy!" she proudly proclaimed to anyone who would listen.

Tom, of course, felt like a million dollars as his daughter paraded him about and introduced him to everyone. She couldn't tell people everything there was to know about her father, nor could she answer every question they might have had about him, his job, his educational background, or his health history. But that didn't stop her from "showing him off" and proudly proclaiming the most important fact: "Look, everyone, this is my daddy!"

I'm sure you see where I'm going with this. You and I may not be able to answer every question there is about God or about Christ. You may not have read the entire Bible yet or studied theology. But we can still proudly proclaim to people: "Look, everyone, this is my best friend Jesus. He's real and He changed my life."

Eventually, of course, Tom's daughter learned all about her father's job, health history, and educational background. So, too, eventually you and I should learn more about God than we may know now. But that doesn't mean that we have to wait until that point to share Christ with others.

In fact, we don't have a choice. Jesus commands us to tell others about Him. His last words before He ascended to heaven (Matthew 28:19–20) were for us to go and tell others about Him. Aren't you glad someone took the time to tell you?

So how do we do that?

Let me suggest a few important steps to take. The first is the most important and in some ways the easiest: Pray for those you want to come to Christ. I can almost guarantee you that someone was praying for you by name when you became a Christian. Now it's your turn to do the same for someone else! Pray for your best friend, for your parents or siblings. Pray for Christ to reveal Himself to them as He did so to you. But you aren't limited to praying for people you know. You can pray for complete strangers if you feel like the Lord is leading you to do so. Pray for that person you think would be the last person to ever accept Christ. If you pray faithfully for him or her you may very well be surprised what happens! The author J. Sidlow Baxter wrote, "Men may spurn our appeal, reject our message, oppose our arguments, despise our persons, but they are helpless against our prayers." Step one: Pray!

Another helpful thing to do is to invite them to church with you (which, by the way, means you need to be going to church yourself!). You might also want to invite them to any group or meeting whose purpose is to share Christ, like Young Life if you are in high school (younglife.org), Cru if you are in college (cru.org), or The Gathering of Men (thegathering.org) if you are out of school. Those things are a great way to partner with other Christians in presenting Christ to people.

Chuck Sugar wrote a song that summed up well my next point about sharing our faith. In "Mrs. Phillips's Prayer" he wrote,

> *Our lives are a Bible for some folks to see.*
> *I wonder just what they are reading in me?*
> *Are they reading God's mercy and love in my life,*
> *Or do they read pain, jealousy, envy, and strife?*
> *I wonder just what they are reading in me.*

It's a great question. Make sure that your life matches your words.

If you begin to do those things, you will see the Lord use you in the lives of others in exciting ways. Don't keep Christ to yourself!

QUIET TIME

Begin your QT today by reading Mark 4, then answer the questions that follow.

---

4 ¶ AGAIN HE began to teach beside the sea. And a very large crowd gathered about him, so that he got into a boat and sat in it on the sea, and the whole crowd was beside the sea on the land.

² And he was teaching them many things in parables, and in his teaching he said to them:

³ "Listen! A sower went out to sow.

⁴ And as he sowed, some seed fell along the path, and the birds came and devoured it.

⁵ Other seed fell on rocky ground, where it did not have much soil, and immediately it sprang up, since it had no depth of soil.

⁶ And when the sun rose it was scorched, and since it had no root, it withered away.

⁷ Other seed fell among thorns, and the thorns grew up and choked it, and it yielded no grain.

⁸ And other seeds fell into good soil and produced grain, growing up and increasing and yielding thirtyfold and sixtyfold and a hundredfold."

⁹ And he said, "He who has ears to hear, let him hear."

¹⁰ ¶ And when he was alone, those around him with the twelve asked him about the parables.

¹¹ And he said to them, "To you has been given the secret of the kingdom of God, but for those outside everything is in parables,

¹² so that "they may indeed see but not perceive, and may indeed hear but not understand, lest they should turn and be forgiven."

¹³ And he said to them, "Do you not understand this parable? How then will you understand all the parables?

¹⁴ The sower sows the word.

¹⁵ And these are the ones along the path, where the word is sown: when they hear, Satan immediately comes and takes away the word that is sown in them.

¹⁶ And these are the ones sown on rocky ground: the ones who, when they hear the word, immediately receive it with joy.

¹⁷ And they have no root in themselves, but endure for a while; then, when tribulation or persecution arises on account of the word, immediately they fall away.

¹⁸ And others are the ones sown among thorns. They are those who hear the word,

¹⁹ but the cares of the world and the deceitfulness of riches and the desires for other things enter in and choke the word, and it proves unfruitful.

²⁰ But those that were sown on the good soil are the ones who hear the word and accept it and bear fruit, thirtyfold and sixtyfold and a hundredfold."

²¹ ¶ And he said to them, "Is a lamp brought in to be put under a basket, or under a bed, and not on a stand?

²² For nothing is hidden except to be made manifest; nor is anything secret except to come to light.

²³ If anyone has ears to hear, let him hear."

²⁴ And he said to them, "Pay attention to what you hear: with the measure you use, it will be measured to you, and still more will be added to you.

²⁵ For to the one who has, more will be given, and from the one who has not, even what he has will be taken away."

²⁶ ¶ And he said, "The kingdom of God is as if a man should scatter seed on the ground.

²⁷ He sleeps and rises night and day, and the seed sprouts and grows; he knows not how.

²⁸ The earth produces by itself, first the blade, then the ear, then the full grain in the ear.

²⁹ But when the grain is ripe, at once he puts in the sickle, because the harvest has come."

³⁰ ¶ And he said, "With what can we compare the kingdom of God, or what parable shall we use for it?

[31] It is like a grain of mustard seed, which, when sown on the ground, is the smallest of all the seeds on earth,

[32] yet when it is sown it grows up and becomes larger than all the garden plants and puts out large branches, so that the birds of the air can make nests in its shade."

[33] ¶ With many such parables he spoke the word to them, as they were able to hear it.

[34] He did not speak to them without a parable, but privately to his own disciples he explained everything.

[35] ¶ On that day, when evening had come, he said to them, "Let us go across to the other side."

[36] And leaving the crowd, they took him with them in the boat, just as he was. And other boats were with him.

[37] And a great windstorm arose, and the waves were breaking into the boat, so that the boat was already filling.

[38] But he was in the stern, asleep on the cushion. And they woke him and said to him, "Teacher, do you not care that we are perishing?"

[39] And he awoke and rebuked the wind and said to the sea, "Peace! Be still!" And the wind ceased, and there was a great calm.

[40] He said to them, "Why are you so afraid? Have you still no faith?"

⁴¹ And they were filled with great fear and said to one another, "Who then is this, that even wind and sea obey him?"

QUESTIONS

As you read the parable of the sower in verses 1–20, ask the Lord to help you be productive and fruitful for Him.

Continue to pray for your non-Christian friends you listed earlier.

Review your list from yesterday's Quiet Time and ask the Lord for His help in those areas in your life.

Begin keeping a list of prayer requests, and keep praying for those things until you see God's answer (usually His answers will either be a "Yes," a "No," or "Wait"). There is nothing too small to pray about, nor is there anything too large. God loves hearing the concerns and details of our lives!

Here is a list of ten, but feel free to make it much longer—

1. _____

2. _____

3. _____

4. _____

5. _____

6. _____

7. _____

8. _____

9. _____

10. _____

As always, end by thanking the Lord for all that He has done and is doing in your life, and for giving you a relationship with Christ.

Now that you have had several Quiet Times you're getting the hang of it. There are still several days' worth of Quiet Times in here, but my commentary will be shorter because you know what to do now.

Remember to keep praying for your friends and family, confessing your sins and asking the Lord's forgiveness, and also thanking Him for who He is and what He does for us. And while you're at it, make sure to pray for our nation, its leaders, and those in authority over you—always a good thing to do.

~

Let every person be subject to the governing authorities. For there is no authority except from God, and those that exist have been instituted by God.

—Romans 13:1

DAY 7

Begin your QT today by reading Mark 5, then answer the questions that follow.

---

5 ¶ THEY CAME to the other side of the sea, to the country of the Gerasenes.

² And when Jesus had stepped out of the boat, immediately there met him out of the tombs a man with an unclean spirit.

³ He lived among the tombs. And no one could bind him anymore, not even with a chain,

⁴ for he had often been bound with shackles and chains, but he wrenched the chains apart, and he broke the shackles in pieces. No one had the strength to subdue him.

⁵ Night and day among the tombs and on the mountains he was always crying out and bruising himself with stones.

⁶ And when he saw Jesus from afar, he ran and fell down before him.

⁷ And crying out with a loud voice, he said, "What have you to do with me, Jesus, Son of the Most High God? I adjure you by God, do not torment me."

Day 7

8 For he was saying to him, "Come out of the man, you unclean spirit!"

9 And Jesus asked him, "What is your name?" He replied, "My name is Legion, for we are many."

10 And he begged him earnestly not to send them out of the country.

11 Now a great herd of pigs was feeding there on the hillside,

12 and they begged him, saying, "Send us to the pigs; let us enter them."

13 So he gave them permission. And the unclean spirits came out, and entered the pigs, and the herd, numbering about two thousand, rushed down the steep bank into the sea and were drowned in the sea.

14 ¶ The herdsmen fled and told it in the city and in the country. And people came to see what it was that had happened.

15 And they came to Jesus and saw the demon-possessed man, the one who had had the legion, sitting there, clothed and in his right mind, and they were afraid.

16 And those who had seen it described to them what had happened to the demon-possessed man and to the pigs.

17 And they began to beg Jesus to depart from their region.

[18] As he was getting into the boat, the man who had been possessed with demons begged him that he might be with him.

[19] And he did not permit him but said to him, "Go home to your friends and tell them how much the Lord has done for you, and how he has had mercy on you."

[20] And he went away and began to proclaim in the Decapolis how much Jesus had done for him, and everyone marveled.

[21] ¶ And when Jesus had crossed again in the boat to the other side, a great crowd gathered about him, and he was beside the sea.

[22] Then came one of the rulers of the synagogue, Jairus by name, and seeing him, he fell at his feet

[23] and implored him earnestly, saying, "My little daughter is at the point of death. Come and lay your hands on her, so that she may be made well and live."

[24] And he went with him. ¶ And a great crowd followed him and thronged about him.

[25] And there was a woman who had had a discharge of blood for twelve years,

[26] and who had suffered much under many physicians, and had spent all that she had, and was no better but rather grew worse.

²⁷ She had heard the reports about Jesus and came up behind him in the crowd and touched his garment.

²⁸ For she said, "If I touch even his garments, I will be made well."

²⁹ And immediately the flow of blood dried up, and she felt in her body that she was healed of her disease.

³⁰ And Jesus, perceiving in himself that power had gone out from him, immediately turned about in the crowd and said, "Who touched my garments?"

³¹ And his disciples said to him, "You see the crowd pressing around you, and yet you say, 'Who touched me?'"

³² And he looked around to see who had done it.

³³ But the woman, knowing what had happened to her, came in fear and trembling and fell down before him and told him the whole truth.

³⁴ And he said to her, "Daughter, your faith has made you well; go in peace, and be healed of your disease."

³⁵ ¶ While he was still speaking, there came from the ruler's house some who said, "Your daughter is dead. Why trouble the Teacher any further?"

³⁶ But overhearing what they said, Jesus said to the ruler of the synagogue, "Do not fear, only believe."

³⁷ And he allowed no one to follow him except Peter and James and John the brother of James.

³⁸ They came to the house of the ruler of the synagogue, and Jesus saw a commotion, people weeping and wailing loudly.

³⁹ And when he had entered, he said to them, "Why are you making a commotion and weeping? The child is not dead but sleeping."

⁴⁰ And they laughed at him. But he put them all outside and took the child's father and mother and those who were with him and went in where the child was.

⁴¹ Taking her by the hand he said to her, "Talitha cumi," which means, "Little girl, I say to you, arise."

⁴² And immediately the girl got up and began walking (for she was twelve years of age), and they were immediately overcome with amazement.

⁴³ And he strictly charged them that no one should know this, and told them to give her something to eat.

QUESTIONS

There are two stories in this chapter: the story of the man with a demon and the story of a dead girl and a sick woman. Do you relate to any of the characters in those stories? Who and why?

Each of the people in those stories had problems they wanted Jesus to heal. What are three things in your own life that you wish He would make better?

1. _____

2. _____

3. _____

Pray for those things today, and continue to pray through your prayer list.

∼

Therefore, confess your sins to one another and pray for one another, that you may be healed. The prayer of a righteous person has great power as it is working.
—James 5:16

DAY 8

Begin your QT today by reading Mark 6, then answer the questions that follow.

---

6 ¶ HE WENT away from there and came to his hometown, and his disciples followed him.

² And on the Sabbath he began to teach in the synagogue, and many who heard him were astonished, saying, "Where did this man get these things? What is the wisdom given to him? How are such mighty works done by his hands?

³ Is not this the carpenter, the son of Mary and brother of James and Joses and Judas and Simon? And are not his sisters here with us?" And they took offense at him.

⁴ And Jesus said to them, "A prophet is not without honor, except in his hometown and among his relatives and in his own household."

⁵ And he could do no mighty work there, except that he laid his hands on a few sick people and healed them.

⁶ And he marveled because of their unbelief. ¶ And he went about among the villages teaching.

⁷ ¶ And he called the twelve and began to send them out two by two, and gave them authority over the unclean spirits.

⁸ He charged them to take nothing for their journey except a staff—no bread, no bag, no money in their belts—

⁹ but to wear sandals and not put on two tunics.

¹⁰ And he said to them, "Whenever you enter a house, stay there until you depart from there.

¹¹ And if any place will not receive you and they will not listen to you, when you leave, shake off the dust that is on your feet as a testimony against them."

¹² So they went out and proclaimed that people should repent.

¹³ And they cast out many demons and anointed with oil many who were sick and healed them.

¹⁴ ¶ King Herod heard of it, for Jesus' name had become known. Some said, "John the Baptist has been raised from the dead. That is why these miraculous powers are at work in him."

¹⁵ But others said, "He is Elijah." And others said, "He is a prophet, like one of the prophets of old."

¹⁶ But when Herod heard of it, he said, "John, whom I beheaded, has been raised."

¹⁷ For it was Herod who had sent and seized John and

abound him in prison for the sake of Herodias, his brother Philip's wife, because he had married her.

¹⁸ For John had been saying to Herod, "It is not lawful for you to have your brother's wife."

¹⁹ And Herodias had a grudge against him and wanted to put him to death. But she could not,

²⁰ for Herod feared John, knowing that he was a righteous and holy man, and he kept him safe. When he heard him, he was greatly perplexed, and yet he heard him gladly.

²¹ But an opportunity came when Herod on his birthday gave a banquet for his nobles and military commanders and the leading men of Galilee.

²² For when Herodias's daughter came in and danced, she pleased Herod and his guests. And the king said to the girl, "Ask me for whatever you wish, and I will give it to you."

²³ And he vowed to her, "Whatever you ask me, I will give you, up to half of my kingdom."

²⁴ And she went out and said to her mother, "For what should I ask?" And she said, "The head of John the Baptist."

²⁵ And she came in immediately with haste to the king and asked, saying, "I want you to give me at once the head of John the Baptist on a platter."

²⁶ And the king was exceedingly sorry, but because of his oaths and his guests he did not want to break his

word to her.

27 And immediately the king sent an executioner with orders to bring John's head. He went and beheaded him in the prison

28 and brought his head on a platter and gave it to the girl, and the girl gave it to her mother.

29 When his disciples heard of it, they came and took his body and laid it in a tomb.

30 ¶ The apostles returned to Jesus and told him all that they had done and taught.

31 And he said to them, "Come away by yourselves to a desolate place and rest a while." For many were coming and going, and they had no leisure even to eat.

32 And they went away in the boat to a desolate place by themselves.

33 Now many saw them going and recognized them, and they ran there on foot from all the towns and got there ahead of them.

34 When he went ashore he saw a great crowd, and he had compassion on them, because they were like sheep without a shepherd. And he began to teach them many things.

35 And when it grew late, his disciples came to him and said, "This is a desolate place, and the hour is now late.

36 Send them away to go into the surrounding countryside and villages and buy themselves something to eat."

[37] But he answered them, "You give them something to eat." And they said to him, "Shall we go and buy two hundred denarii worth of bread and give it to them to eat?"

[38] And he said to them, "How many loaves do you have? Go and see." And when they had found out, they said, "Five, and two fish."

[39] Then he commanded them all to sit down in groups on the green grass.

[40] So they sat down in groups, by hundreds and by fifties.

[41] And taking the five loaves and the two fish he looked up to heaven and said a blessing and broke the loaves and gave them to the disciples to set before the people. And he divided the two fish among them all.

[42] And they all ate and were satisfied.

[43] And they took up twelve baskets full of broken pieces and of the fish.

[44] And those who ate the loaves were five thousand men.

[45] ¶ Immediately he made his disciples get into the boat and go before him to the other side, to Bethsaida, while he dismissed the crowd.

[46] And after he had taken leave of them, he went up on the mountain to pray.

⁴⁷ And when evening came, the boat was out on the sea, and he was alone on the land.

⁴⁸ And he saw that they were making headway painfully, for the wind was against them. And about the fourth watch of the night he came to them, walking on the sea. He meant to pass by them,

⁴⁹ but when they saw him walking on the sea they thought it was a ghost, and cried out,

⁵⁰ for they all saw him and were terrified. But immediately he spoke to them and said, "Take heart; it is I. Do not be afraid."

⁵¹ And he got into the boat with them, and the wind ceased. And they were utterly astounded,

⁵² for they did not understand about the loaves, but their hearts were hardened.

⁵³ ¶ When they had crossed over, they came to land at Gennesaret and moored to the shore.

⁵⁴ And when they got out of the boat, the people immediately recognized him

⁵⁵ and ran about the whole region and began to bring the sick people on their beds to wherever they heard he was.

⁵⁶ And wherever he came, in villages, cities, or countryside, they laid the sick in the marketplaces and implored him that they might touch even the fringe of his garment. And as many as touched it were made well.

QUESTIONS

In your own words, what happens in the story told in the first six verses of this chapter?

What do you think kept Jesus from being able to heal people there?

Verses 14–29 talk about a guy named John the Baptist. Who was he? See if you can find other places in the Bible that talk about him.

Jesus is very active in this chapter. Which of the miracles talked about in Mark 6 is your favorite? What would it have been like to be there when He did it?

Do you think Jesus is still in the "miracle business" today? I do, and I bet the longer you walk with Him the more you will feel that way, too.

Spend some time thanking Him for being in your life and some time asking Him to be involved in the things you have going on today.

DAY 9

Begin your QT today by reading Mark 7, then answer the questions that follow.

---

7 ¶ NOW WHEN the Pharisees gathered to him, with some of the scribes who had come from Jerusalem,

² they saw that some of his disciples ate with hands that were defiled, that is, unwashed.

³ (For the Pharisees and all the Jews do not eat unless they wash their hands, holding to the tradition of the elders,

⁴ and when they come from the marketplace, they do not eat unless they wash. And there are many other traditions that they observe, such as the washing of cups and pots and copper vessels and dining couches.)

⁵ And the Pharisees and the scribes asked him, "Why do your disciples not walk according to the tradition of the elders, but eat with defiled hands?"

⁶ And he said to them, "Well did Isaiah prophesy of you hypocrites, as it is written,

"'This people honors me with their lips,

but their heart is far from me;

⁷ in vain do they worship me,
teaching as doctrines the
commandments of men.'

⁸ You leave the commandment of God and hold to the tradition of men."

⁹ ¶ And he said to them, "You have a fine way of rejecting the commandment of God in order to establish your tradition!

¹⁰ For Moses said, 'Honor your father and your mother'; and, 'Whoever reviles father or mother must surely die.'

¹¹ But you say, 'If a man tells his father or his mother, Whatever you would have gained from me is Corban' (that is, given to God)—

¹² then you no longer permit him to do anything for his father or mother,

¹³ thus making void the word of God by your tradition that you have handed down. And many such things you do."

¹⁴ ¶ And he called the people to him again and said to them, "Hear me, all of you, and understand:

¹⁵ There is nothing outside a person that by going into him can defile him, but the things that come out of a person are what defile him."

¹⁷ And when he had entered the house and left the

people, his disciples asked him about the parable.

¹⁸ And he said to them, "Then are you also without understanding? Do you not see that whatever goes into a person from outside cannot defile him,

¹⁹ since it enters not his heart but his stomach, and is expelled?" (Thus he declared all foods clean.)

²⁰ And he said, "What comes out of a person is what defiles him.

²¹ For from within, out of the heart of man, come evil thoughts, sexual immorality, theft, murder, adultery,

²² coveting, wickedness, deceit, sensuality, envy, slander, pride, foolishness.

²³ All these evil things come from within, and they defile a person."

²⁴ ¶ And from there he arose and went away to the region of Tyre and Sidon. And he entered a house and did not want anyone to know, yet he could not be hidden.

²⁵ But immediately a woman whose little daughter was possessed by an unclean spirit heard of him and came and fell down at his feet.

²⁶ Now the woman was a Gentile, a Syrophoenician by birth. And she begged him to cast the demon out of her daughter.

²⁷ And he said to her, "Let the children be fed first, for

it is not right to take the children's bread and throw it to the dogs."

²⁸ But she answered him, "Yes, Lord; yet even the dogs under the table eat the children's crumbs."

²⁹ And he said to her, "For this statement you may go your way; the demon has left your daughter."

³⁰ And she went home and found the child lying in bed and the demon gone.

³¹ ¶ Then he returned from the region of Tyre and went through Sidon to the Sea of Galilee, in the region of the Decapolis.

³² And they brought to him a man who was deaf and had a speech impediment, and they begged him to lay his hand on him.

³³ And taking him aside from the crowd privately, he put his fingers into his ears, and after spitting touched his tongue.

³⁴ And looking up to heaven, he sighed and said to him, "Ephphatha," that is, "Be opened."

³⁵ And his ears were opened, his tongue was released, and he spoke plainly.

³⁶ And Jesus charged them to tell no one. But the more he charged them, the more zealously they proclaimed it.

³⁷ And they were astonished beyond measure, saying,

"He has done all things well. He even makes the deaf hear and the mute speak."

QUESTIONS

This chapter may not have been the easiest to understand so far! If you were to break it down into sections, what would they be? (For instance, verses 1–13 talk about traditions and commandments.)

The next section is verses 14–23. What does it talk about?

The other two sections are miracle stories. What are the two miracles?

One of my favorite descriptions of Jesus occurs at the end of this chapter. Take a look at the last verse in this chapter. How does it say Jesus does things?

Everything Jesus does, He does well, or with excellence. That includes the work He is doing in your life. Philippians 1:6 tells us, "I am sure of this, that he who began a good work in you will bring it to completion at the day of Jesus Christ."

Do you remember the lists you made earlier of your friends to pray for and things to be thankful for? Remember to keep praying for those things.

~

He told them a parable to the effect that they ought always to pray and not lose heart.

—Luke 18:1

DAY 10

Begin your QT today by reading Mark 8, then answer the questions that follow.

---

8 ¶ IN THOSE days, when again a great crowd had gathered, and they had nothing to eat, he called his disciples to him and said to them,

2 "I have compassion on the crowd, because they have been with me now three days and have nothing to eat.

3 And if I send them away hungry to their homes, they will faint on the way. And some of them have come from far away."

4 And his disciples answered him, "How can one feed these people with bread here in this desolate place?"

5 And he asked them, "How many loaves do you have?" They said, "Seven."

6 And he directed the crowd to sit down on the ground. And he took the seven loaves, and having given thanks, he broke them and gave them to his disciples to set before the people; and they set them before the crowd.

7 And they had a few small fish. And having blessed

them, he said that these also should be set before them.

[8] And they ate and were satisfied. And they took up the broken pieces left over, seven baskets full.

[9] And there were about four thousand people. And he sent them away.

[10] And immediately he got into the boat with his disciples and went to the district of Dalmanutha.

[11] ¶ The Pharisees came and began to argue with him, seeking from him a sign from heaven to test him.

[12] And he sighed deeply in his spirit and said, "Why does this generation seek a sign? Truly, I say to you, no sign will be given to this generation."

[13] And he left them, got into the boat again, and went to the other side.

[14] ¶ Now they had forgotten to bring bread, and they had only one loaf with them in the boat.

[15] And he cautioned them, saying, "Watch out; beware of the leaven of the Pharisees and the leaven of Herod."

[16] And they began discussing with one another the fact that they had no bread.

[17] And Jesus, aware of this, said to them, "Why are you discussing the fact that you have no bread? Do you not yet perceive or understand? Are your hearts hardened?

¹⁸ Having eyes do you not see, and having ears do you not hear? And do you not remember?

¹⁹ When I broke the five loaves for the five thousand, how many baskets full of broken pieces did you take up?" They said to him, "Twelve."

²⁰ "And the seven for the four thousand, how many baskets full of broken pieces did you take up?" And they said to him, "Seven."

²¹ And he said to them, "Do you not yet understand?"

²² ¶ And they came to Bethsaida. And some people brought to him a blind man and begged him to touch him.

²³ And he took the blind man by the hand and led him out of the village, and when he had spit on his eyes and laid his hands on him, he asked him, "Do you see anything?"

²⁴ And he looked up and said, "I see men, but they look like trees, walking."

²⁵ Then Jesus laid his hands on his eyes again; and he opened his eyes, his sight was restored, and he saw everything clearly.

²⁶ And he sent him to his home, saying, "Do not even enter the village."

²⁷ ¶ And Jesus went on with his disciples to the villages of Caesarea Philippi. And on the way he asked

his disciples, "Who do people say that I am?"

28 And they told him, "John the Baptist; and others say, Elijah; and others, one of the prophets."

29 And he asked them, "But who do you say that I am?" Peter answered him, "You are the Christ."

30 And he strictly charged them to tell no one about him.

31 ¶ And he began to teach them that the Son of Man must suffer many things and be rejected by the elders and the chief priests and the scribes and be killed, and after three days rise again.

32 And he said this plainly. And Peter took him aside and began to rebuke him.

33 But turning and seeing his disciples, he rebuked Peter and said, "Get behind me, Satan! For you are not setting your mind on the things of God, but on the things of man."

34 ¶ And he called to him the crowd with his disciples and said to them, "If anyone would come after me, let him deny himself and take up his cross and follow me.

35 For whoever would save his life will lose it, but whoever loses his life for my sake and the gospel's will save it.

36 For what does it profit a man to gain the whole world and forfeit his life?

³⁷ For what can a man give in return for his life?

³⁸ For whoever is ashamed of me and of my words in this adulterous and sinful generation, of him will the Son of Man also be ashamed when he comes in the glory of his Father with the holy angels."

QUESTIONS

You can probably see why I suggested you start your walk with Christ by reading the Gospel of Mark. It's such a great story and there's action on every page. Mark 8 is certainly a good example of that.

Compare the feeding of 4,000 in this chapter with the feeding of 5,000 in chapter 6. What are the similarities? What are the differences?

Peter was a great follower of Jesus and this chapter tells of an important event in his life. What was it?

In your own life, when was the time that you said, "You are the Christ"?

Lastly, what do verses 34–35 mean to you?

~

I have been crucified with Christ. It is no longer I who live, but Christ who lives in me. And the life I now live in the flesh I live by faith in the Son of God, who loved me and gave himself for me.

—Galatians 2:20

DAY 11

Begin your QT today by reading Mark 9, then answer the questions that follow.

---

9 ¶ AND HE said to them, "Truly, I say to you, there are some standing here who will not taste death until they see the kingdom of God after it has come with power."

² ¶ And after six days Jesus took with him Peter and James and John, and led them up a high mountain by themselves. And he was transfigured before them,

³ and his clothes became radiant, intensely white, as no one on earth could bleach them.

⁴ And there appeared to them Elijah with Moses, and they were talking with Jesus.

⁵ And Peter said to Jesus, "Rabbi, it is good that we are here. Let us make three tents, one for you and one for Moses and one for Elijah."

⁶ For he did not know what to say, for they were terrified.

⁷ And a cloud overshadowed them, and a voice came out of the cloud, "This is my beloved Son; listen to him."

⁸ And suddenly, looking around, they no longer saw anyone with them but Jesus only.

⁹ ¶ And as they were coming down the mountain, he charged them to tell no one what they had seen, until the Son of Man had risen from the dead.

¹⁰ So they kept the matter to themselves, questioning what this rising from the dead might mean.

¹¹ And they asked him, "Why do the scribes say that first Elijah must come?"

¹² And he said to them, "Elijah does come first to restore all things. And how is it written of the Son of Man that he should suffer many things and be treated with contempt?

¹³ But I tell you that Elijah has come, and they did to him whatever they pleased, as it is written of him."

¹⁴ ¶ And when they came to the disciples, they saw a great crowd around them, and scribes arguing with them.

¹⁵ And immediately all the crowd, when they saw him, were greatly amazed and ran up to him and greeted him.

¹⁶ And he asked them, "What are you arguing about with them?"

¹⁷ And someone from the crowd answered him, "Teacher, I brought my son to you, for he has a spirit that makes him mute.

¹⁸ And whenever it seizes him, it throws him down, and he foams and grinds his teeth and becomes rigid. So I asked your disciples to cast it out, and they were not able."

¹⁹ And he answered them, "O faithless generation, how long am I to be with you? How long am I to bear with you? Bring him to me."

²⁰ And they brought the boy to him. And when the spirit saw him, immediately it convulsed the boy, and he fell on the ground and rolled about, foaming at the mouth.

²¹ And Jesus asked his father, "How long has this been happening to him?" And he said, "From childhood.

²² And it has often cast him into fire and into water, to destroy him. But if you can do anything, have compassion on us and help us."

²³ And Jesus said to him, "If you can! All things are possible for one who believes."

²⁴ Immediately the father of the child cried out and said, "I believe; help my unbelief!"

²⁵ And when Jesus saw that a crowd came running together, he rebuked the unclean spirit, saying to it, "You mute and deaf spirit, I command you, come out of him and never enter him again."

²⁶ And after crying out and convulsing him terribly, it came out, and the boy was like a corpse, so that most

of them said, "He is dead."

²⁷ But Jesus took him by the hand and lifted him up, and he arose.

²⁸ And when he had entered the house, his disciples asked him privately, "Why could we not cast it out?"

²⁹ And he said to them, "This kind cannot be driven out by anything but prayer."

³⁰ ¶ They went on from there and passed through Galilee. And he did not want anyone to know,

³¹ for he was teaching his disciples, saying to them, "The Son of Man is going to be delivered into the hands of men, and they will kill him. And when he is killed, after three days he will rise."

³² But they did not understand the saying, and were afraid to ask him.

³³ ¶ And they came to Capernaum. And when he was in the house he asked them, "What were you discussing on the way?"

³⁴ But they kept silent, for on the way they had argued with one another about who was the greatest.

³⁵ And he sat down and called the twelve. And he said to them, "If anyone would be first, he must be last of all and servant of all."

³⁶ And he took a child and put him in the midst of them, and taking him in his arms, he said to them,

³⁷ "Whoever receives one such child in my name receives me, and whoever receives me, receives not me but him who sent me."

³⁸ ¶ John said to him, "Teacher, we saw someone casting out demons in your name, and we tried to stop him, because he was not following us."

³⁹ But Jesus said, "Do not stop him, for no one who does a mighty work in my name will be able soon afterward to speak evil of me.

⁴⁰ For the one who is not against us is for us.

⁴¹ For truly, I say to you, whoever gives you a cup of water to drink because you belong to Christ will by no means lose his reward.

⁴² ¶ "Whoever causes one of these little ones who believe in me to sin, it would be better for him if a great millstone were hung around his neck and he were thrown into the sea.

⁴³ And if your hand causes you to sin, cut it off. It is better for you to enter life crippled than with two hands to go to hell, to the unquenchable fire.

⁴⁵ And if your foot causes you to sin, cut it off. It is better for you to enter life lame than with two feet to be thrown into hell.

⁴⁷ And if your eye causes you to sin, tear it out. It is better for you to enter the kingdom of God with one eye than with two eyes to be thrown into hell,

⁴⁸ 'where their worm does not die and the fire is not quenched.'

⁴⁹ For everyone will be salted with fire.

⁵⁰ Salt is good, but if the salt has lost its saltiness, how will you make it salty again? Have salt in yourselves, and be at peace with one another."

QUESTIONS

This first part of this chapter tells of the Transfiguration. The dictionary defines *transfiguration* as "a complete change of form or appearance into a more beautiful or spiritual state." What would it have been like to be with Jesus during this event?

In verses 30–32 what does Jesus tell His disciples? Can you see why the disciples did not understand Him?

What does the fact that Jesus knew what was going to happen to Him mean? Can you think why that might be significant? (Hint: It has to do with the fact that He went willingly.)

Take a look at verses 33–35. What are some ways you can be more of a servant in your own life?

Lastly, spend some time today asking the Lord to reveal to you the things in your life that He would like to change. Ask Him for the ability and strength to change those things.

～

No temptation has overtaken you that is not common to man. God is faithful, and he will not let you be tempted beyond your ability, but with the temptation he will also provide the way of escape, that you may be able to endure it.

—1 Corinthians 10:13

DAY 12

Begin your QT today by reading Mark 10, then answer the questions that follow.

---

10 ¶ AND HE left there and went to the region of Judea and beyond the Jordan, and crowds gathered to him again. And again, as was his custom, he taught them.

² ¶ And Pharisees came up and in order to test him asked, "Is it lawful for a man to divorce his wife?"

³ He answered them, "What did Moses command you?"

⁴ They said, "Moses allowed a man to write a certificate of divorce and to send her away."

⁵ And Jesus said to them, "Because of your hardness of heart he wrote you this commandment.

⁶ But from the beginning of creation, 'God made them male and female.'

⁷ 'Therefore a man shall leave his father and mother and hold fast to his wife,

⁸ and they shall become one flesh.' So they are no longer two but one flesh.

⁹ What therefore God has joined together, let not man separate."

¹⁰ ¶ And in the house the disciples asked him again about this matter.

¹¹ And he said to them, "Whoever divorces his wife and marries another commits adultery against her,

¹² and if she divorces her husband and marries another, she commits adultery."

¹³ ¶ And they were bringing children to him that he might touch them, and the disciples rebuked them.

¹⁴ But when Jesus saw it, he was indignant and said to them, "Let the children come to me; do not hinder them, for to such belongs the kingdom of God.

¹⁵ Truly, I say to you, whoever does not receive the kingdom of God like a child shall not enter it."

¹⁶ And he took them in his arms and blessed them, laying his hands on them.

¹⁷ ¶ And as he was setting out on his journey, a man ran up and knelt before him and asked him, "Good Teacher, what must I do to inherit eternal life?"

¹⁸ And Jesus said to him, "Why do you call me good? No one is good except God alone.

¹⁹ You know the commandments: 'Do not murder, Do not commit adultery, Do not steal, Do not bear false witness, Do not defraud, Honor your father and mother.'"

²⁰ And he said to him, "Teacher, all these I have kept from my youth."

²¹ And Jesus, looking at him, loved him, and said to him, "You lack one thing: go, sell all that you have and give to the poor, and you will have treasure in heaven; and come, follow me."

²² Disheartened by the saying, he went away sorrowful, for he had great possessions.

²³ ¶ And Jesus looked around and said to his disciples, "How difficult it will be for those who have wealth to enter the kingdom of God!"

²⁴ And the disciples were amazed at his words. But Jesus said to them again, "Children, how difficult it is to enter the kingdom of God!

²⁵ It is easier for a camel to go through the eye of a needle than for a rich person to enter the kingdom of God."

²⁶ And they were exceedingly astonished, and said to him, "Then who can be saved?"

²⁷ Jesus looked at them and said, "With man it is impossible, but not with God. For all things are possible with God."

²⁸ Peter began to say to him, "See, we have left everything and followed you."

²⁹ Jesus said, "Truly, I say to you, there is no one who has left house or brothers or sisters or mother or

father or children or lands, for my sake and for the gospel,

³⁰ who will not receive a hundredfold now in this time, houses and brothers and sisters and mothers and children and lands, with persecutions, and in the age to come eternal life.

³¹ But many who are first will be last, and the last first."

³² ¶ And they were on the road, going up to Jerusalem, and Jesus was walking ahead of them. And they were amazed, and those who followed were afraid. And taking the twelve again, he began to tell them what was to happen to him,

³³ saying, "See, we are going up to Jerusalem, and the Son of Man will be delivered over to the chief priests and the scribes, and they will condemn him to death and deliver him over to the Gentiles.

³⁴ And they will mock him and spit on him, and flog him and kill him. And after three days he will rise."

³⁵ ¶ And James and John, the sons of Zebedee, came up to him and said to him, "Teacher, we want you to do for us whatever we ask of you."

³⁶ And he said to them, "What do you want me to do for you?"

³⁷ And they said to him, "Grant us to sit, one at your right hand and one at your left, in your glory."

³⁸ Jesus said to them, "You do not know what you are asking. Are you able to drink the cup that I drink, or to be baptized with the baptism with which I am baptized?"

³⁹ And they said to him, "We are able." And Jesus said to them, "The cup that I drink you will drink, and with the baptism with which I am baptized, you will be baptized,

⁴⁰ but to sit at my right hand or at my left is not mine to grant, but it is for those for whom it has been prepared."

⁴¹ And when the ten heard it, they began to be indignant at James and John.

⁴² And Jesus called them to him and said to them, "You know that those who are considered rulers of the Gentiles lord it over them, and their great ones exercise authority over them.

⁴³ But it shall not be so among you. But whoever would be great among you must be your servant,

⁴⁴ and whoever would be first among you must be slave of all.

⁴⁵ For even the Son of Man came not to be served but to serve, and to give his life as a ransom for many."

⁴⁶ ¶ And they came to Jericho. And as he was leaving Jericho with his disciples and a great crowd, Bartimaeus, a blind beggar, the son of Timaeus, was sitting by the roadside.

⁴⁷ And when he heard that it was Jesus of Nazareth, he began to cry out and say, "Jesus, Son of David, have mercy on me!"

⁴⁸ And many rebuked him, telling him to be silent. But he cried out all the more, "Son of David, have mercy on me!"

⁴⁹ And Jesus stopped and said, "Call him." And they called the blind man, saying to him, "Take heart. Get up; he is calling you."

⁵⁰ And throwing off his cloak, he sprang up and came to Jesus.

⁵¹ And Jesus said to him, "What do you want me to do for you?" And the blind man said to him, "Rabbi, let me recover my sight."

⁵² And Jesus said to him, "Go your way; your faith has made you well." And immediately he recovered his sight and followed him on the way.

QUESTIONS

Based on what you have read in this chapter, what did Jesus think about marriage? Re-read the first twelve verses if you're not sure. What do those verses tell you about sex outside of marriage?

Verses 13–16 paint a familiar picture of Jesus. In your own words, what happened in that story? What does it mean to have "childlike" faith?

Another very famous Gospel story is the one that follows in verses 17–31, commonly known as "The Rich Young Man" or "The Rich Young Ruler." Why does the rich young man go away sad?

How are you like the rich young man? How are you different?

What are some things that are difficult for you to give up to Jesus?

Later in this chapter, what do James and John ask of Jesus? What is His response?

Finally, in the first ten chapters of Mark you have seen many miracles, including the one at the end of this chapter. What part did faith play in all of those miracles?

Go back to Mark 9 and pray what the father prayed in verse 24.

DAY 13

We're going to do something different for the next several days, rather than continuing in the Gospel of Mark. Don't worry—we'll get back to Mark shortly, and by the time you have finished this book you will have read the entire Gospel.

It's a good idea to put a little variety into your Quiet Times. You don't want to get stuck in a rut. After all, you don't do the exact same things with your best friend every day, do you? In the same way, it's good to "mix things up" in your Quiet Time occasionally. With that in mind, we're going to spend the next few days looking at God's character.

While at first this might seem to have nothing to do with Mark, you will see that it helps the Gospel make even more sense.

Look at Psalm 145:3:

> Great is the LORD, and greatly to be praised,
> and his greatness is unsearchable.

What does that verse tell us about God?

It reminds us that God is "unsearchable"—that His greatness cannot be fully understood by us. We serve an awesome God. And while He is too great for our little minds to completely comprehend, we can know some things about Him. We'll look at a few of those things in the days ahead.

Read Psalm 98:

1   Oh sing to the LORD a new song,
         for he has done marvelous
            things!
     His right hand and his holy arm
         have worked salvation for him.

2   The LORD has made known his
            salvation;
         he has revealed his
            righteousness in the sight of
            the nations.

3   He has remembered his steadfast
            love and faithfulness
         to the house of Israel.
     All the ends of the earth have seen
         the salvation of our God.

4   ¶ Make a joyful noise to the LORD,
            all the earth;
         break forth into joyous song and
            sing praises!

5   Sing praises to the LORD with the
      lyre,
      with the lyre and the sound of
      melody!

6   With trumpets and the sound of
      the horn
      make a joyful noise before the
      King, the LORD!

7   ¶ Let the sea roar, and all that fills
      it;
      the world and those who dwell
      in it!

8   Let the rivers clap their hands;
      let the hills sing for joy together

9   before the LORD, for he comes
      to judge the earth.
      He will judge the world with
      righteousness,
      and the peoples with equity.

QUESTIONS

Spend the rest of this Quiet Time doing the things that Psalm 98 tells us to do. Give thanks and praise to God for what you know about Him.

List seven things about God that you think are awesome. Use the Bible (the Psalms especially) if you get stumped:

1. _____

2. _____

3. _____

4. _____

5. _____

6. _____

7. _____

Don't forget to pray for the things you have been praying for regularly.

DAY 14

Let's continue with our study on God's character.

What do you think God is like? Is He friendly? Is He awe-inspiring? Is He harsh? Does He make mistakes? Does He sin?

Read Psalm 100. It's short, only five verses.

1   Make a joyful noise to the LORD, all
         the earth!
2   Serve the LORD with gladness!
         Come into his presence with
         singing!
3   ¶ Know that the LORD, he is God!
         It is he who made us, and we
            are his;
         we are his people, and the sheep
            of his pasture.
4   ¶ Enter his gates with thanksgiving,
         and his courts with praise!
         Give thanks to him; bless his
            name!
5   ¶ For the LORD is good;
         his steadfast love endures
            forever,
         and his faithfulness to all
            generations.

QUESTIONS

Take a look at the last verse. What does it say about God?

This verse, and many others like it, makes a simple statement about God: "The Lord is good."

Think about that for a moment. What does it mean to be truly good? Don't confuse it with the idea of good-better-best, where good is only so-so. In the Bible, good means morally perfect. You can't get any better.

Go back to Mark 10 and read verse 18. What does Jesus say about good in that passage?

(By the way, Jesus was not denying that He is God, He was just reminding His questioner that only God—and by extension, Jesus Himself—is truly good.)

Sometimes we forget that God is different than we are. But He is. Why should we be *glad* that God is good?

Why should we be *troubled* that God is good? (Hint: True goodness cannot tolerate anything less than good.)

Spend some time praying for your friends, family, and thanking God for His goodness.

DAY 15

Yesterday we looked at the fact that God is good. Today we're going to see one of the benefits of that goodness.

Read Psalm 23. (It's one of the most famous chapters in the entire Bible, by the way, and you might have heard it before.)

1   The LORD is my shepherd; I shall
        not want.
2   He makes me lie down in green
        pastures.
    He leads me beside still waters.
3   He restores my soul.
    He leads me in paths of
        righteousness
        for his name's sake.
4   ¶ Even though I walk through the
        valley of the shadow of death,
        I will fear no evil,
    for you are with me;
        your rod and your staff,
        they comfort me.
5   ¶ You prepare a table before me
        in the presence of my enemies;

you anoint my head with oil;
my cup overflows.
6   Surely goodness and mercy shall
follow me
all the days of my life,
and I shall dwell in the house of the
LORD forever.

Now take a look at Psalm 18:30:

This God—his way is perfect;
the word of the LORD proves
true;
he is a shield for all those who
take refuge in him.

What does Psalm 18:30 tell us about God?

His way is _____.

His Word is _____.

What does a shield do? What, then, does that
mean about God?

Here's how I would summarize this verse and
this attribute of God: He is totally worthy of our
trust. Think about that. What does that mean?

Among other things it means that when God does something or says something, we can put our trust in it. He is not like anyone else you know. He is totally worthy of our trust. Even your family, as great as they are, might fail you at some point. Not God.

Pray for some things in your life and the lives of those you know where God's help is needed, and thank Him for being trustworthy.

DAY 16

We have seen that God is good and that He is trustworthy. Let's consider a third aspect of His character.

God is self-sufficient.

What does that mean?

Look at Acts 17:24–25 below. What does this tell us about God?

> The God who made the world and everything in it, being Lord of heaven and earth, does not live in temples made by man, nor is he served by human hands, as though he needed anything, since he himself gives to all mankind life and breath and everything.

You can see by that verse that God does not need us. He loves us, yes, but He does not need us. We, on the other hand, are anything but self-sufficient. We need the Lord, first of all. We also need family and friends and associates.

Read Isaiah 40:12–17. It gives a striking image of the self-sufficiency and power of God.

12   ¶ Who has measured the waters in
      the hollow of his hand
      and marked off the heavens with
      a span,
    enclosed the dust of the earth in a
      measure
      and weighed the mountains in
      scales
      and the hills in a balance?

13   Who has measured the Spirit of the
      LORD,
      or what man shows him his
      counsel?

14   Whom did he consult,
      and who made him understand?
    Who taught him the path of justice,
      and taught him knowledge,
      and showed him the way of
      understanding?

15   Behold, the nations are like a drop
      from a bucket,
      and are accounted as the dust
      on the scales;
      behold, he takes up the
      coastlands like fine dust.

¹⁶ Lebanon would not suffice for fuel,
    nor are its beasts enough for a
        burnt offering.
¹⁷ All the nations are as nothing
        before him,
    they are accounted by him
        as less than nothing and
            emptiness.

The passage uses a technique of asking rhetorical questions. Those are questions that aren't really meant to get an answer, but to make you think. List three of the questions this passage asks about God:

1. _____

2. _____

3. _____

In each case, the idea is that no one or no thing is greater than the Lord, nor helped Him to become what He is.

Spend some time acknowledging to the Lord that you need Him.

DAY 17

God is good. He is trustworthy. He is self-sufficient. We have one more aspect of His character and an aspect of our own character to look at before we dive into the rest of Mark's Gospel.

First, the final characteristic of God's character: God is love.

Read 1 John 4:7–8 (note: that's First John—a short letter near the end of the New Testament, not the Gospel of John):

> Beloved, let us love one another, for love is from God, and whoever loves has been born of God and knows God. Anyone who does not love does not know God, because God is love.

Isn't it great that we serve a God who is loving? Yes, He is morally perfect and without sin, but He is also loving. Here's a great way to describe His love for us: *He always wants what's best for us.*

Think about that: Because God loves us, He *always* wants what's best for us. Not necessarily what's easiest or most pleasant, but what is best.

Now look at another passage in 1 John, chapter 1:5–6:

> This is the message we have heard from him and proclaim to you, that God is light, and in him is no darkness at all. If we say we have fellowship with him while we walk in darkness, we lie and do not practice the truth.

In the Bible, "darkness" is a metaphor for sin. God has no sin in Him. In fact, just as in life, where light (God) exists, there can be no darkness (sin). That means that you and I have a problem. We are sinful (see Romans 3:10–12), and God by His very nature cannot tolerate sin.

You might already see where this is going, but if you do not, don't worry, because in the final chapters of Mark you will see how God provided the perfect solution to our problem. A way for two aspects of His character—His love and His righteousness—to be satisfied without compromising His character.

Spend a few minutes thinking about the following questions:

What is good about light?

What is bad about darkness?

What is good about love?

Finish your devotional by spending some time with the Lord and bringing to Him the things that are on your heart today.

DAY 18

The final chapters of Mark are going to bring together those aspects of God's character that we have been studying. A refresher before we continue:

God is good.

God is trustworthy.

God is self-sufficient (He doesn't need us or anyone else).

God is love.

Now let's get back to Mark. Read Mark 11, then answer the questions that follow.

---

11 ¶ NOW WHEN they drew near to Jerusalem, to Bethphage and Bethany, at the Mount of Olives, Jesus sent two of his disciples

² and said to them, "Go into the village in front of you, and immediately as you enter it you will find a colt tied, on which no one has ever sat. Untie it and bring it.

³ If anyone says to you, 'Why are you doing this?' say, 'The Lord has need of it and will send it back here immediately.' "

⁴ And they went away and found a colt tied at a door outside in the street, and they untied it.

⁵ And some of those standing there said to them, "What are you doing, untying the colt?"

⁶ And they told them what Jesus had said, and they let them go.

⁷ And they brought the colt to Jesus and threw their cloaks on it, and he sat on it.

⁸ And many spread their cloaks on the road, and others spread leafy branches that they had cut from the fields.

⁹ And those who went before and those who followed were shouting, "Hosanna! Blessed is he who comes in the name of the Lord!

¹⁰ Blessed is the coming kingdom of our father David! Hosanna in the highest!"

¹¹ ¶ And he entered Jerusalem and went into the temple. And when he had looked around at everything, as it was already late, he went out to Bethany with the twelve.

¹² ¶ On the following day, when they came from Bethany, he was hungry.

¹³ And seeing in the distance a fig tree in leaf, he went to see if he could find anything on it. When he came to it, he found nothing but leaves, for it was not the season for figs.

¹⁴ And he said to it, "May no one ever eat fruit from you again." And his disciples heard it.

¹⁵ ¶ And they came to Jerusalem. And he entered the temple and began to drive out those who sold and those who bought in the temple, and he overturned the tables of the money-changers and the seats of those who sold pigeons.

¹⁶ And he would not allow anyone to carry anything through the temple.

¹⁷ And he was teaching them and saying to them, "Is it not written, 'My house shall be called a house of prayer for all the nations'? But you have made it a den of robbers."

¹⁸ And the chief priests and the scribes heard it and were seeking a way to destroy him, for they feared him, because all the crowd was astonished at his teaching.

¹⁹ And when evening came they went out of the city.

²⁰ ¶ As they passed by in the morning, they saw the fig tree withered away to its roots.

²¹ And Peter remembered and said to him, "Rabbi, look! The fig tree that you cursed has withered."

²² And Jesus answered them, "Have faith in God.

²³ Truly, I say to you, whoever says to this mountain, 'Be taken up and thrown into the sea,' and does not doubt in his heart, but believes that what he says will come to pass, it will be done for him.

²⁴ Therefore I tell you, whatever you ask in prayer, believe that you have received it, and it will be yours.

²⁵ And whenever you stand praying, forgive, if you have anything against anyone, so that your Father also who is in heaven may forgive you your trespasses."

²⁷ ¶ And they came again to Jerusalem. And as he was walking in the temple, the chief priests and the scribes and the elders came to him,

²⁸ and they said to him, "By what authority are you doing these things, or who gave you this authority to do them?"

²⁹ Jesus said to them, "I will ask you one question; answer me, and I will tell you by what authority I do these things.

³⁰ Was the baptism of John from heaven or from man? Answer me."

³¹ And they discussed it with one another, saying, "If we say, 'From heaven,' he will say, 'Why then did you not believe him?'

³² But shall we say, 'From man'?"—they were afraid

of the people, for they all held that John really was a prophet.

33 So they answered Jesus, "We do not know." And Jesus said to them, "Neither will I tell you by what authority I do these things."

QUESTIONS

In all four Gospels—Matthew, Mark, Luke, and John—lots of time is spent on just one week in Jesus' life, His final week on earth. The fact that they all spend so much time on it tells us that it must be significant.

Look in the other Gospels and see if you can find the story of Jesus' last week. What chapters talk about Jesus' last week in Matthew? _____ In Luke? _____ In John? _____.

What city do those events take place in?

Why did Jesus do what He did to the fig tree?

Chapter 11 ends with Jesus' authority questioned. Where did Jesus' authority come from?

DAY 19

Read Mark 12, then answer the questions that follow.

---

12 ¶ AND HE began to speak to them in parables. "A man planted a vineyard and put a fence around it and dug a pit for the winepress and built a tower, and leased it to tenants and went into another country.

² When the season came, he sent a servant to the tenants to get from them some of the fruit of the vineyard.

³ And they took him and beat him and sent him away empty-handed.

⁴ Again he sent to them another servant, and they struck him on the head and treated him shamefully.

⁵ And he sent another, and him they killed. And so with many others: some they beat, and some they killed.

⁶ He had still one other, a beloved son. Finally he sent him to them, saying, 'They will respect my son.'

⁷ But those tenants said to one another, 'This is the heir. Come, let us kill him, and the inheritance will be ours.'

⁸ And they took him and killed him and threw him out of the vineyard.

⁹ What will the owner of the vineyard do? He will come and destroy the tenants and give the vineyard to others.

¹⁰ Have you not read this Scripture:

> "'The stone that the builders
>   rejected
>   has become the cornerstone;
> ¹¹ this was the Lord's doing,
>   and it is marvelous in our
>   eyes'?"

¹² ¶ And they were seeking to arrest him but feared the people, for they perceived that he had told the parable against them. So they left him and went away.

¹³ ¶ And they sent to him some of the Pharisees and some of the Herodians, to trap him in his talk.

¹⁴ And they came and said to him, "Teacher, we know that you are true and do not care about anyone's opinion. For you are not swayed by appearances, but truly teach the way of God. Is it lawful to pay taxes to Caesar, or not? Should we pay them, or should we not?"

¹⁵ But, knowing their hypocrisy, he said to them, "Why put me to the test? Bring me a denarius and let me look at it."

¹⁶ And they brought one. And he said to them, "Whose likeness and inscription is this?" They said to him, "Caesar's."

¹⁷ Jesus said to them, "Render to Caesar the things that are Caesar's, and to God the things that are God's." And they marveled at him.

¹⁸ ¶ And Sadducees came to him, who say that there is no resurrection. And they asked him a question, saying,

¹⁹ "Teacher, Moses wrote for us that if a man's brother dies and leaves a wife, but leaves no child, the man must take the widow and raise up offspring for his brother.

²⁰ There were seven brothers; the first took a wife, and when he died left no offspring.

²¹ And the second took her, and died, leaving no offspring. And the third likewise.

²² And the seven left no offspring. Last of all the woman also died.

²³ In the resurrection, when they rise again, whose wife will she be? For the seven had her as wife."

²⁴ ¶ Jesus said to them, "Is this not the reason you are wrong, because you know neither the Scriptures nor the power of God?

²⁵ For when they rise from the dead, they neither marry nor are given in marriage, but are like angels in heaven.

²⁶ And as for the dead being raised, have you not read in the book of Moses, in the passage about the bush, how God spoke to him, saying, 'I am the God of Abraham, and the God of Isaac, and the God of Jacob'?

²⁷ He is not God of the dead, but of the living. You are quite wrong."

²⁸ ¶ And one of the scribes came up and heard them disputing with one another, and seeing that he answered them well, asked him, "Which commandment is the most important of all?"

²⁹ Jesus answered, "The most important is, 'Hear, O Israel: The Lord our God, the Lord is one.

³⁰ And you shall love the Lord your God with all your heart and with all your soul and with all your mind and with all your strength.'

³¹ The second is this: 'You shall love your neighbor as yourself.' There is no other commandment greater than these."

³² And the scribe said to him, "You are right, Teacher. You have truly said that he is one, and there is no other besides him.

³³ And to love him with all the heart and with all the understanding and with all the strength, and to love one's neighbor as oneself, is much more than all whole burnt offerings and sacrifices."

³⁴ And when Jesus saw that he answered wisely, he

said to him, "You are not far from the kingdom of God." And after that no one dared to ask him any more questions.

[35] ¶ And as Jesus taught in the temple, he said, "How can the scribes say that the Christ is the son of David?

[36] David himself, in the Holy Spirit, declared,

> "'The Lord said to my Lord,
> Sit at my right hand,
>   until I put your enemies under
>   your feet.'

[37] David himself calls him Lord. So how is he his son?" And the great throng heard him gladly.

[38] ¶ And in his teaching he said, "Beware of the scribes, who like to walk around in long robes and like greetings in the marketplaces

[39] and have the best seats in the synagogues and the places of honor at feasts,

[40] who devour widows' houses and for a pretense make long prayers. They will receive the greater condemnation."

[41] ¶ And he sat down opposite the treasury and watched the people putting money into the offering box. Many rich people put in large sums.

[42] And a poor widow came and put in two small copper coins, which make a penny.

⁴³ And he called his disciples to him and said to them, "Truly, I say to you, this poor widow has put in more than all those who are contributing to the offering box.

⁴⁴ For they all contributed out of their abundance, but she out of her poverty has put in everything she had, all she had to live on."

QUESTIONS

What do you think is the point of the story about paying taxes to Caesar?

In verses 28–34 Jesus talks about the Great Commandment. What does He say is the greatest commandment?

Looking at your own life, how do you do with obeying that commandment? Have you seen positive progress in that since you became a Christian?

What can you do today to improve on loving the Lord—

• with all your soul? _____

• with all your mind? _____

• with all your strength? _____

Work on those things today and pray for the Lord to help you do so.

Lastly, why did Jesus consider the widow's gift better than the others? Why should we be generous? Can you think of some ways that you can begin to give of yourself in a sacrificial way?

DAY 20

Read Mark 13, then answer the questions that follow.

---

13 ¶ AND AS he came out of the temple, one of his disciples said to him, "Look, Teacher, what wonderful stones and what wonderful buildings!"

² And Jesus said to him, "Do you see these great buildings? There will not be left here one stone upon another that will not be thrown down."

³ ¶ And as he sat on the Mount of Olives opposite the temple, Peter and James and John and Andrew asked him privately,

⁴ "Tell us, when will these things be, and what will be the sign when all these things are about to be accomplished?"

⁵ And Jesus began to say to them, "See that no one leads you astray.

⁶ Many will come in my name, saying, 'I am he!' and they will lead many astray.

⁷ And when you hear of wars and rumors of wars, do not be alarmed. This must take place, but the end is not yet.

[8] For nation will rise against nation, and kingdom against kingdom. There will be earthquakes in various places; there will be famines. These are but the beginning of the birth pains.

[9] ¶ "But be on your guard. For they will deliver you over to councils, and you will be beaten in synagogues, and you will stand before governors and kings for my sake, to bear witness before them.

[10] And the gospel must first be proclaimed to all nations.

[11] And when they bring you to trial and deliver you over, do not be anxious beforehand what you are to say, but say whatever is given you in that hour, for it is not you who speak, but the Holy Spirit.

[12] And brother will deliver brother over to death, and the father his child, and children will rise against parents and have them put to death.

[13] And you will be hated by all for my name's sake. But the one who endures to the end will be saved.

[14] ¶ "But when you see the abomination of desolation standing where it ought not to be (let the reader understand), then let those who are in Judea flee to the mountains.

[15] Let the one who is on the housetop not go down, nor enter his house, to take anything out,

[16] and let the one who is in the field not turn back to take his cloak.

¹⁷ And alas for women who are pregnant and for those who are nursing infants in those days!

¹⁸ Pray that it may not happen in winter.

¹⁹ For in those days there will be such tribulation as has not been from the beginning of the creation that God created until now, and never will be.

²⁰ And if the Lord had not cut short the days, no human being would be saved. But for the sake of the elect, whom he chose, he shortened the days.

²¹ And then if anyone says to you, 'Look, here is the Christ!' or 'Look, there he is!' do not believe it.

²² False christs and false prophets will arise and perform signs and wonders, to lead astray, if possible, the elect.

²³ But be on guard; I have told you all things beforehand.

²⁴ ¶ "But in those days, after that tribulation, the sun will be darkened, and the moon will not give its light,

²⁵ and the stars will be falling from heaven, and the powers in the heavens will be shaken.

²⁶ And then they will see the Son of Man coming in clouds with great power and glory.

²⁷ And then he will send out the angels and gather his elect from the four winds, from the ends of the earth to the ends of heaven.

²⁸ ¶ "From the fig tree learn its lesson: as soon as its branch becomes tender and puts out its leaves, you know that summer is near.

²⁹ So also, when you see these things taking place, you know that he is near, at the very gates.

³⁰ Truly, I say to you, this generation will not pass away until all these things take place.

³¹ Heaven and earth will pass away, but my words will not pass away.

³² ¶ "But concerning that day or that hour, no one knows, not even the angels in heaven, nor the Son, but only the Father.

³³ Be on guard, keep awake. For you do not know when the time will come.

³⁴ It is like a man going on a journey, when he leaves home and puts his servants in charge, each with his work, and commands the doorkeeper to stay awake.

³⁵ Therefore stay awake—for you do not know when the master of the house will come, in the evening, or at midnight, or when the cock crows, or in the morning—

³⁶ lest he come suddenly and find you asleep.

³⁷ And what I say to you I say to all: Stay awake."

QUESTIONS

This chapter talks a lot about the end of the world as we know it. For decades movies and books have been written about the way the world will end. The difference between them and the Bible is that the Bible actually knows how it's going to end.

Why do you think Jesus thought it was important to tell His friends about the future?

List several things that this chapter tells you about the way the world is going to end.

_____

_____

_____

_____

_____

_____

Pray for the people and things on your heart.

DAY 21

Read the first half of Mark 14, then answer the questions that follow.

14 ¶ IT WAS now two days before the Passover and the Feast of Unleavened Bread. And the chief priests and the scribes were seeking how to arrest him by stealth and kill him,

2 for they said, "Not during the feast, lest there be an uproar from the people."

3 ¶ And while he was at Bethany in the house of Simon the leper, as he was reclining at table, a woman came with an alabaster flask of ointment of pure nard, very costly, and she broke the flask and poured it over his head.

4 There were some who said to themselves indignantly, "Why was the ointment wasted like that?

5 For this ointment could have been sold for more than three hundred denarii and given to the poor." And they scolded her.

6 But Jesus said, "Leave her alone. Why do you trouble her? She has done a beautiful thing to me.

7 For you always have the poor with you, and when-

ever you want, you can do good for them. But you will not always have me.

⁸ She has done what she could; she has anointed my body beforehand for burial.

⁹ And truly, I say to you, wherever the gospel is proclaimed in the whole world, what she has done will be told in memory of her."

¹⁰ ¶ Then Judas Iscariot, who was one of the twelve, went to the chief priests in order to betray him to them.

¹¹ And when they heard it, they were glad and promised to give him money. And he sought an opportunity to betray him.

¹² ¶ And on the first day of Unleavened Bread, when they sacrificed the Passover lamb, his disciples said to him, "Where will you have us go and prepare for you to eat the Passover?"

¹³ And he sent two of his disciples and said to them, "Go into the city, and a man carrying a jar of water will meet you. Follow him,

¹⁴ and wherever he enters, say to the master of the house, 'The Teacher says, Where is my guest room, where I may eat the Passover with my disciples?'

¹⁵ And he will show you a large upper room furnished and ready; there prepare for us."

¹⁶ And the disciples set out and went to the city and

found it just as he had told them, and they prepared the Passover.

¹⁷ ¶ And when it was evening, he came with the twelve.

¹⁸ And as they were reclining at table and eating, Jesus said, "Truly, I say to you, one of you will betray me, one who is eating with me."

¹⁹ They began to be sorrowful and to say to him one after another, "Is it I?"

²⁰ He said to them, "It is one of the twelve, one who is dipping bread into the dish with me.

²¹ For the Son of Man goes as it is written of him, but woe to that man by whom the Son of Man is betrayed! It would have been better for that man if he had not been born."

²² ¶ And as they were eating, he took bread, and after blessing it broke it and gave it to them, and said, "Take; this is my body."

²³ And he took a cup, and when he had given thanks he gave it to them, and they all drank of it.

²⁴ And he said to them, "This is my blood of the covenant, which is poured out for many.

²⁵ Truly, I say to you, I will not drink again of the fruit of the vine until that day when I drink it new in the kingdom of God."

²⁶ ¶ And when they had sung a hymn, they went out to the Mount of Olives.

²⁷ And Jesus said to them, "You will all fall away, for it is written, 'I will strike the shepherd, and the sheep will be scattered.'

²⁸ But after I am raised up, I will go before you to Galilee."

²⁹ Peter said to him, "Even though they all fall away, I will not."

³⁰ And Jesus said to him, "Truly, I tell you, this very night, before the rooster crows twice, you will deny me three times."

³¹ But he said emphatically, "If I must die with you, I will not deny you." And they all said the same.

³² ¶ And they went to a place called Gethsemane. And he said to his disciples, "Sit here while I pray."

³³ And he took with him Peter and James and John, and began to be greatly distressed and troubled.

³⁴ And he said to them, "My soul is very sorrowful, even to death. Remain here and watch."

³⁵ And going a little farther, he fell on the ground and prayed that, if it were possible, the hour might pass from him.

³⁶ And he said, "Abba, Father, all things are possible for you. Remove this cup from me. Yet not what I will, but what you will."

³⁷ And he came and found them sleeping, and he

said to Peter, "Simon, are you asleep? Could you not watch one hour?

[38] Watch and pray that you may not enter into temptation. The spirit indeed is willing, but the flesh is weak."

[39] And again he went away and prayed, saying the same words.

[40] And again he came and found them sleeping, for their eyes were very heavy, and they did not know what to answer him.

[41] And he came the third time and said to them, "Are you still sleeping and taking your rest? It is enough; the hour has come. The Son of Man is betrayed into the hands of sinners.

[42] Rise, let us be going; see, my betrayer is at hand."

QUESTIONS

The events of the final week are beginning to speed up and this chapter sets the stage for the remaining days of Jesus' earthly life.

Who was plotting to kill Jesus?

Even though they were doing the plotting, for whom did Jesus actually die?

Day 21

What was the gift of the woman in verses 3–9?

Who betrayed Jesus?

The Passover was a celebration of God's deliverance of the Jews from slavery. (Extra points if you can research and find some of the significant parallels between Passover and Christ's death. See Exodus 12 for the Passover story.)

With whom was Jesus celebrating Passover?

Jesus introduced a new tradition the night of the Last Supper, one that all Christian churches still follow. Do you know what it is? (It's talked about in verses 22–25.)

Who does Jesus predict is going to deny Him? How many times is he going to deny Him?

Thank the Lord for all He has done for you. Ask Him to help you stay loyal to Him and never betray or deny Him. Pray, too, for your friends and family.

DAY 22

Read the rest of Mark 14, then answer the questions that follow.

14⁴³ ¶ AND immediately, while he was still speaking, Judas came, one of the twelve, and with him a crowd with swords and clubs, from the chief priests and the scribes and the elders.

⁴⁴ Now the betrayer had given them a sign, saying, "The one I will kiss is the man. Seize him and lead him away under guard."

⁴⁵ And when he came, he went up to him at once and said, "Rabbi!" And he kissed him.

⁴⁶ And they laid hands on him and seized him.

⁴⁷ But one of those who stood by drew his sword and struck the servant of the high priest and cut off his ear.

⁴⁸ And Jesus said to them, "Have you come out as against a robber, with swords and clubs to capture me?

⁴⁹ Day after day I was with you in the temple teaching, and you did not seize me. But let the Scriptures be fulfilled."

⁵⁰ And they all left him and fled.

⁵¹ ¶ And a young man followed him, with nothing but a linen cloth about his body. And they seized him,

⁵² but he left the linen cloth and ran away naked.

⁵³ ¶ And they led Jesus to the high priest. And all the chief priests and the elders and the scribes came together.

⁵⁴ And Peter had followed him at a distance, right into the courtyard of the high priest. And he was sitting with the guards and warming himself at the fire.

⁵⁵ Now the chief priests and the whole Council were seeking testimony against Jesus to put him to death, but they found none.

⁵⁶ For many bore false witness against him, but their testimony did not agree.

⁵⁷ And some stood up and bore false witness against him, saying,

⁵⁸ "We heard him say, 'I will destroy this temple that is made with hands, and in three days I will build another, not made with hands.' "

⁵⁹ Yet even about this their testimony did not agree.

⁶⁰ And the high priest stood up in the midst and asked Jesus, "Have you no answer to make? What is it that these men testify against you?"

⁶¹ But he remained silent and made no answer. Again

the high priest asked him, "Are you the Christ, the Son of the Blessed?"

⁶² And Jesus said, "I am, and you will see the Son of Man seated at the right hand of Power, and coming with the clouds of heaven."

⁶³ And the high priest tore his garments and said, "What further witnesses do we need?

⁶⁴ You have heard his blasphemy. What is your decision?" And they all condemned him as deserving death.

⁶⁵ And some began to spit on him and to cover his face and to strike him, saying to him, "Prophesy!" And the guards received him with blows.

⁶⁶ ¶ And as Peter was below in the courtyard, one of the servant girls of the high priest came,

⁶⁷ and seeing Peter warming himself, she looked at him and said, "You also were with the Nazarene, Jesus."

⁶⁸ But he denied it, saying, "I neither know nor understand what you mean." And he went out into the gateway and the rooster crowed.

⁶⁹ And the servant girl saw him and began again to say to the bystanders, "This man is one of them."

⁷⁰ But again he denied it. And after a little while the bystanders again said to Peter, "Certainly you are one of them, for you are a Galilean."

⁷¹ But he began to invoke a curse on himself and to swear, "I do not know this man of whom you speak."

⁷² And immediately the rooster crowed a second time. And Peter remembered how Jesus had said to him, "Before the rooster crows twice, you will deny me three times." And he broke down and wept.

QUESTIONS

What evidence is there in this chapter that Jesus went to His death willingly?

What evidence is there in this chapter that, though He went willingly, it was still difficult for Him to do?

Make sure to thank the Lord again today for what He went through for you on the night of His betrayal.

Today would be a great time to spend time praying for your friends who have not come to understand the significance of Christ's sacrifice for them. Spend some time praying for those friends and thanking Jesus for what He did for you on the cross.

DAY 23

Read Mark 15, then answer the questions that follow.

---

15 ¶ AND AS soon as it was morning, the chief priests held a consultation with the elders and scribes and the whole Council. And they bound Jesus and led him away and delivered him over to Pilate.

² And Pilate asked him, "Are you the King of the Jews?" And he answered him, "You have said so."

³ And the chief priests accused him of many things.

⁴ And Pilate again asked him, "Have you no answer to make? See how many charges they bring against you."

⁵ But Jesus made no further answer, so that Pilate was amazed.

⁶ ¶ Now at the feast he used to release for them one prisoner for whom they asked.

⁷ And among the rebels in prison, who had committed murder in the insurrection, there was a man called Barabbas.

⁸ And the crowd came up and began to ask Pilate to do as he usually did for them.

⁹ And he answered them, saying, "Do you want me to release for you the King of the Jews?"

¹⁰ For he perceived that it was out of envy that the chief priests had delivered him up.

¹¹ But the chief priests stirred up the crowd to have him release for them Barabbas instead.

¹² And Pilate again said to them, "Then what shall I do with the man you call the King of the Jews?"

¹³ And they cried out again, "Crucify him."

¹⁴ And Pilate said to them, "Why, what evil has he done?" But they shouted all the more, "Crucify him."

¹⁵ So Pilate, wishing to satisfy the crowd, released for them Barabbas, and having scourged Jesus, he delivered him to be crucified.

¹⁶ ¶ And the soldiers led him away inside the palace (that is, the governor's headquarters), and they called together the whole battalion.

¹⁷ And they clothed him in a purple cloak, and twisting together a crown of thorns, they put it on him.

¹⁸ And they began to salute him, "Hail, King of the Jews!"

¹⁹ And they were striking his head with a reed and spitting on him and kneeling down in homage to him.

²⁰ And when they had mocked him, they stripped him of the purple cloak and put his own clothes on him. And they led him out to crucify him.

²¹ ¶ And they compelled a passerby, Simon of Cyrene, who was coming in from the country, the father of Alexander and Rufus, to carry his cross.

²² And they brought him to the place called Golgotha (which means Place of a Skull).

²³ And they offered him wine mixed with myrrh, but he did not take it.

²⁴ And they crucified him and divided his garments among them, casting lots for them, to decide what each should take.

²⁵ And it was the third hour when they crucified him.

²⁶ And the inscription of the charge against him read, "The King of the Jews."

²⁷ And with him they crucified two robbers, one on his right and one on his left.

²⁹ And those who passed by derided him, wagging their heads and saying, "Aha! You who would destroy the temple and rebuild it in three days,

³⁰ save yourself, and come down from the cross!"

³¹ So also the chief priests with the scribes mocked him to one another, saying, "He saved others; he cannot save himself.

³² Let the Christ, the King of Israel, come down now from the cross that we may see and believe." Those who were crucified with him also reviled him.

³³ ¶ And when the sixth hour had come, there was darkness over the whole land until the ninth hour.

³⁴ And at the ninth hour Jesus cried with a loud voice, "Eloi, Eloi, lema sabachthani?" which means, "My God, my God, why have you forsaken me?"

³⁵ And some of the bystanders hearing it said, "Behold, he is calling Elijah."

³⁶ And someone ran and filled a sponge with sour wine, put it on a reed and gave it to him to drink, saying, "Wait, let us see whether Elijah will come to take him down."

³⁷ And Jesus uttered a loud cry and breathed his last.

³⁸ And the curtain of the temple was torn in two, from top to bottom.

³⁹ And when the centurion, who stood facing him, saw that in this way he breathed his last, he said, "Truly this man was the Son of God!"

⁴⁰ ¶ There were also women looking on from a distance, among whom were Mary Magdalene, and Mary the mother of James the younger and of Joses, and Salome.

⁴¹ When he was in Galilee, they followed him and ministered to him, and there were also many other women who came up with him to Jerusalem.

⁴² ¶ And when evening had come, since it was the day of Preparation, that is, the day before the Sabbath,

⁴³ Joseph of Arimathea, a respected member of the Council, who was also himself looking for the kingdom of God, took courage and went to Pilate and asked for the body of Jesus.

⁴⁴ Pilate was surprised to hear that he should have already died. And summoning the centurion, he asked him whether he was already dead.

⁴⁵ And when he learned from the centurion that he was dead, he granted the corpse to Joseph.

⁴⁶ And Joseph bought a linen shroud, and taking him down, wrapped him in the linen shroud and laid him in a tomb that had been cut out of the rock. And he rolled a stone against the entrance of the tomb.

⁴⁷ Mary Magdalene and Mary the mother of Joses saw where he was laid.

QUESTIONS

Who was Pilate?

Who was the man that was released instead of Jesus?

Re-read verses 16–20. How do they make you feel?

Who was crucified along with Jesus?

What does Jesus cry out in verse 34? Read Psalm 22:1–2 and you will see that Jesus was quoting the Bible:

> 1   My God, my God, why have you
>   forsaken me?
>   Why are you so far from saving
>   me, from the words of my
>   groaning?
> 2   O my God, I cry by day, but you do
>   not answer,
>   and by night, but I find no rest.

What is the significance of those words?

What did Jesus' death on the cross accomplish? Read Romans 5:6–8:

> For while we were still weak, at the right time Christ died for the ungodly. For one will scarcely die for a righteous person—though perhaps for a good person one would dare even to die—but God shows his love for us in that while we were still sinners, Christ died for us.

If you have never done so, thank Jesus for dying for your sins on the cross. If you would like to begin a relationship with Him, there is no better time than now. (Go back to page 14 for a prayer that will help you do just that.) If you have already begun a relationship with Christ, tell Him again how much your appreciate all He has done for you.

Spend some time praying for your friends and family that they may begin to understand God's tremendous love for them in Christ.

~

Therefore, if anyone is in Christ, he is a new creation. The old has passed away; behold, the new has come.
—2 Corinthians 5:17

DAY 24

Today's Quiet Time is our last one. We'll finish up the Gospel of Mark with a very important chapter, Mark 16.

---

16 ¶ WHEN THE Sabbath was past, Mary Magdalene and Mary the mother of James and Salome bought spices, so that they might go and anoint him.

² And very early on the first day of the week, when the sun had risen, they went to the tomb.

³ And they were saying to one another, "Who will roll away the stone for us from the entrance of the tomb?"

⁴ And looking up, they saw that the stone had been rolled back—it was very large.

⁵ And entering the tomb, they saw a young man sitting on the right side, dressed in a white robe, and they were alarmed.

⁶ And he said to them, "Do not be alarmed. You seek Jesus of Nazareth, who was crucified. He has risen; he is not here. See the place where they laid him.

⁷ But go, tell his disciples and Peter that he is going

before you to Galilee. There you will see him, just as he told you."

⁸ And they went out and fled from the tomb, for trembling and astonishment had seized them, and they said nothing to anyone, for they were afraid.

[Some of the earliest manuscripts do not include 16:9–20.]

⁹ ¶ [[Now when he rose early on the first day of the week, he appeared first to Mary Magdalene, from whom he had cast out seven demons.

¹⁰ She went and told those who had been with him, as they mourned and wept.

¹¹ But when they heard that he was alive and had been seen by her, they would not believe it.

¹² ¶ After these things he appeared in another form to two of them, as they were walking into the country.

¹³ And they went back and told the rest, but they did not believe them.

¹⁴ ¶ Afterward he appeared to the eleven themselves as they were reclining at table, and he rebuked them for their unbelief and hardness of heart, because they had not believed those who saw him after he had risen.

¹⁵ And he said to them, "Go into all the world and proclaim the gospel to the whole creation.

¹⁶ Whoever believes and is baptized will be saved, but whoever does not believe will be condemned.

¹⁷ And these signs will accompany those who believe: in my name they will cast out demons; they will speak in new tongues;

¹⁸ they will pick up serpents with their hands; and if they drink any deadly poison, it will not hurt them; they will lay their hands on the sick, and they will recover."

¹⁹ ¶ So then the Lord Jesus, after he had spoken to them, was taken up into heaven and sat down at the right hand of God.

²⁰ And they went out and preached everywhere, while the Lord worked with them and confirmed the message by accompanying signs.]]

QUESTIONS

The fact that Jesus rose from the dead is of wonderful significance! Among other things it's what gives us the ability to have a personal relationship with Him now. He's still alive!

Several days ago we took a detour from Mark and studied a few aspects of God's character. Among other things, the Bible tells us that,

—God is good.

—God is trustworthy.

—God is self-sufficient (He doesn't need us or anyone else).

—God is love.

(Remember that Jesus, the Father, and the Spirit all have the same qualities.)

Can you begin to see how these attributes came into play in the death and resurrection of Jesus?

His moral perfection or absolute goodness means that He cannot tolerate sin. Since we've all sinned, that presents a real problem for us. The fact that He is trustworthy means that we can depend completely on what He says. The fact that He is good also means that He would never go back on His promises, giving us yet another reason to know He is trustworthy. The fact that He is self-sufficient reminds us that God does not need us; instead He chooses us out of love.

Finally, the fact that He is love explains why He would go to the lengths He has in order to allow us into a relationship with Him. God is amazing, isn't He?

John 3:16 may be the most famous verse in the Bible. That's in large part because it sums up the gospel so well: "For God so loved the world, that he gave his only Son, that whoever believes in him should not perish but have eternal life."

Yesterday you read a few verses from the fifth chapter of Romans. Now read a few more—look at Romans 5:6–11:

> For while we were still weak, at the right time Christ died for the ungodly. For one will scarcely die for a righteous person— though perhaps for a good person one would dare even to die—but God shows his love for us in that while we were still sinners, Christ died for us. Since, therefore, we have now been justified by his blood, much more shall we be saved by him from the wrath of God. For if while we were enemies we were reconciled to God by the death of his Son, much more, now that we are reconciled, shall we be saved by his life. More than that, we also rejoice in God through our Lord Jesus Christ, through whom we have now received reconciliation.

Spend some time reflecting on all that you have learned over these last few weeks. Also spend some time praying for all the various people and things the Lord has put on your heart.

IN CONCLUSION

We've reached the end of this little book. I hope you've enjoyed it and that it has helped you take your first steps with Christ.

Keep having these daily "QTs." Now that you've read all of Mark, use the Bible reading chart in the back of this book for a suggested order to read through the rest of the New Testament.

If, in your daily readings, you come upon something you don't understand, talk to your pastor or an older Christian friend and ask him or her what they think. Keep praying for your friends, family, and those who don't know Christ, and keep looking for ways to make your life more Christ-like.

An analogy that seems very fitting to our relationship with Jesus is marriage. There is a courtship period (which for you may have been like the period when you first heard about Jesus). That's followed by a wedding where the couple commits themselves to each other (which is like giving your life to Christ and becoming a Christian). Then there's the honeymoon period (which is a lot like the first few days after you become a Christian).

Wouldn't it be tragic if a newlywed couple separated just after they got home from their honeymoon? And yet that's what happens with many new Christians. After the "honeymoon" they decide that "it's just not the same as it was at first" and they put their faith on hold.

The key to successful marriages is love. And love is more than just an ooey-gooey feeling. Love is a commitment to one another through thick and thin. Love is unconditional. Love is difficult. But it is also what makes relationships work.

Fall in love with Jesus.

Put into practice the things we have talked about over these pages—having a daily devotional time with Him, spending time with other Christians, obeying what you read in Scripture, going to church, being accountable to other believers, sharing your faith with others. Learn to do those things even when you don't feel like it; even when it's not fun. If you think marriage is always fun, you haven't talked to many married people! Even the best marriages take work.

Becoming a Christian is one of the easiest things you could ever do: Christ has done all the work for you; you merely need to respond in faith. But *being* a Christian—like marriage—is difficult. But it's worth it!

You were made for one thing: to know Jesus. Your life will only be all that it can be if you are rightly related to Him and living for Him. If you do that, the best part of life isn't the time before you became a Christian or even that moment you did—it's the rest of your life, lived in a growing relationship with the One who cares more for you than anyone else in the world does.

Enjoy the adventure!

ABOUT THE AUTHOR

Kit Sublett lives in Houston where he served on the staff of Young Life, a ministry to high school students, for twenty years. He is a graduate of Trinity University. Kit is the youngest of seven siblings, uncle to thirteen, and great-uncle to twelve (and counting).

COLOPHON

Cover designed by Stephanie Whitlock Dicken

Book designed by Randolph McMann for Whitecaps Media

Body text is set in Scala and Scala Sans, fonts designed by Martin Majoor. Titles are set in Flood Std

Printing by Bang Printing, Brainerd, Minnesota

BIBLE READING CHART

This Bible Reading Chart was designed to help you read the Bible. Rather than read the New Testament in the order shown in the table of contents, many people have found it more profitable and enjoyable to read it in this order, which spreads out the types of books so that the Gospels are intermingled with the epistles and the shorter books are mixed in with the longer ones.

Simply cross off the chapters as you read them. You've already completed Mark. Before long you will have read through the entire New Testament!

BIBLE READING CHART by Kit

Book	Chapters Read
MARK	1 2 3 4 5 6 7 8 9 10 11 12 13 14 15 16
1 JOHN	1 2 3 4 5
COLOSSIANS	1 2 3 4
JOHN	1 2 3 4 5 6 7 8 9 10 11 12 13 14 15 16 17 18 19 20 21
JAMES	1 2 3 4 5
PHILEMON	1
1 TIMOTHY	1 2 3 4 5 6
2 TIMOTHY	1 2 3 4
PHILIPPIANS	1 2 3 4
HEBREWS	1 2 3 4 5 6 7 8 9 10 11 12 13
1 THESSALONIANS	1 2 3 4 5
2 THESSALONIANS	1 2 3
MATTHEW	1 2 3 4 5 6 7 8 9 10 11 12 13 14 15 16 17 18 19 20 21 22 23 24 25 26 27 28
2 JOHN	1
3 JOHN	1
JUDE	1
ROMANS	1 2 3 4 5 6 7 8 9 10 11 12 13 14 15 16
TITUS	1 2 3
ACTS	1 2 3 4 5 6 7 8 9 10 11 12 13 14 15 16 17 18 19 20 21 22 23 24 25 26 27 28
1 PETER	1 2 3 4 5
2 PETER	1 2 3
1 CORINTHIANS	1 2 3 4 5 6 7 8 9 10 11 12 13 14 15 16
EPHESIANS	1 2 3 4 5 6
LUKE	1 2 3 4 5 6 7 8 9 10 11 12 13 14 15 16 17 18 19 20 21 22 23 24
GALATIANS	1 2 3 4 5 6
2 CORINTHIANS	1 2 3 4 5 6 7 8 9 10 11 12 13
REVELATION	1 2 3 4 5 6 7 8 9 10 11 12 13 14 15 16 17 18 19 20 21 22

© 1992 Kit Sublett

NOTES

NOTES

NOTES

NOTES

By the same author ...

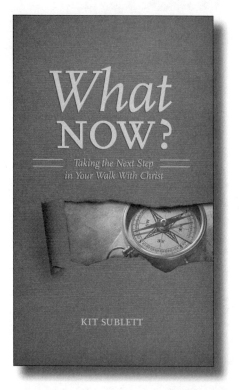

What Now? Taking the Next Step in Your Walk with Christ is the perfect follow-up to *The Adventure Begins.*

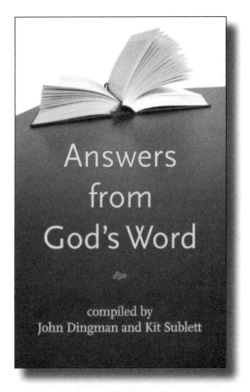

Find out what the Bible has to say about dozens
of topics in *Answers from God's Word*.

These books and other great titles are available at
whitecapsmedia.com or ask for them from your
favorite bookseller!